PRAISE FOR *TOWARD BEAUTY*

"This book is a triumph. Garnhum's journey of discovery is a journey for us all. Within these pages lies a message of hope—a message we all need to receive. We are worthy of a life of beauty, a life of creativity, a life of love. *Toward Beauty* is a gentle act of kindness, for all of us."

—Dan Mullins, host of *My Camino: The Podcast*

"Reading *Toward Beauty* is a form of self-care: It offers laughter, meditation, and release. Without the worry of boarding passes or blisters, all you have to do is surrender to the writing for its buoyancy and charm. Through his artful observations and genuine vulnerability, Garnhum invites the reader to escape to this sun-drenched world and contemplate their own tough questions."

—Winnie Yeung, award-winning coauthor of *Homes: A Refugee Story*

"This book is for people—like me—who love to travel. Garnhum's ability to tell a clear and simple story made me feel as if I were actually walking beside him in northern Spain."

—Ali Velshi, journalist at MSNBC and host of *Velshi*

"Lace up some comfortable shoes and prepare to be taken on an extraordinary adventure. *Toward Beauty* is armchair travel at its finest. And as with every truly meaningful journey, we are richer and wiser for having taken the trip."

—Gill Deacon, author and broadcaster

"*Toward Beauty* reveals the passions, joys, and wounds that a life in the theatre can bring. Garnhum's honesty is devastating and inspiring and, yes, . . . beautiful."
—Antoni Cimolino, artistic director of the Stratford Festival

"Honest, wry, and poignant, *Toward Beauty* will grab you by the heart and mind and drag you laughing and crying on this captivating journey of body and soul. Luminous."
—Shelley Ambrose, former publisher of *The Walrus*

"We all need this book! A singular pilgrimage to collectively share as we all attempt to reconnect our lives to the spirit to actually live them. *Toward Beauty* is the escape and understanding I crave. Like hanging out with a best friend who just gets the struggle and beauty of living now, who takes you to your own dark corners of existence and blows in the wind, lets in the sun, and pours the wine."
—Jennifer Clement, head of acting at Vancouver Film School

"Moving and witty, *Toward Beauty* is a poignant reminder that inner change is the path that really matters. . . . And while that journey is solitary, our fellow pilgrims make all the difference."
—Amanda Lang, host of *Taking Stock* on CTV

"*Toward Beauty* is a book full of wonder, humor, grief, and discovery and will speak to anyone who has struggled to find joy in the darkness. A delicious and deeply moving story!"
—Carey Perloff, artistic director emerita at the American
Conservatory Theater

"This delightful travelogue is beautiful, playful, thoughtful, vulnerable, and full of surprises . . . a testament to the present—and the presence of others—both of which make life worth living. . . . [This] book is for anyone who seeks beauty and a better future."

—Rick Miller, performer, writer, and director

TOWARD
BEAUTY

TOWARD BEAUTY

REIGNITING A CREATIVE LIFE ON THE CAMINO DE SANTIAGO

DENNIS GARNHUM

COMPASS
PRESS

Published by Compass Press, Toronto

Edited and designed by Girl Friday Productions
www.girlfridayproductions.com

Cover design: Emily Weigel
Project management: Emilie Sandoz-Voyer
Image credits: cover © Shutterstock/Forgem
Photo of author by Dahlia Katz

ISBN (paperback): 978-1-7782653-0-3
ISBN (e-book): 978-1-7782653-1-0

To those walking the path, asking the questions.

BEFORE

WALK SOFTLY

THE SEAT BELT SIGN TURNS OFF. I stand and stretch my weary legs after my long flight across the Atlantic Ocean. I had plenty of room on this half-full flight, but sleeping awkwardly on two airline seats with a mask across my mouth doesn't equal a good night's rest. I pull down my knapsack from the luggage compartment, its weight propelling it to descend quickly into the aisle. I lift my right leg onto an empty seat. Grabbing the brand-new backpack, I hoist it up to my awaiting knee, slip one arm into a strap, and then the other. At thirty-five pounds, it's a rather heavy load I'm lifting. Inside my bag is everything I'll need to endure a lengthy and challenging hike in the heat of the summer sun.

I exit the airplane and walk down the long boxy jetway, emerging into the centre of the Madrid airport terminal. The building gleams with polished wood, soaring arches, and glass walls.

After a moment, I notice my surroundings more closely. What should be a busy, crowded space has a rather ghost town–like atmosphere. Empty gates and closed restaurants. Stores with metal barriers that are lowered and locked. The

3

airport is practically abandoned and underutilized. Yellow tape lines cover every second chair to remind people to keep their distance from each other—a useless gesture. Almost no one is here.

Today's journey is not over—I have one short flight later, after a six-hour layover here. Tomorrow I begin walking the Camino del Norte in northeastern Spain, which clocks in at a terrifying 830 kilometres.

WHEN I TOLD PEOPLE I was about to run off to Spain to hike alone for over a month—in the midst of a global pandemic—I received the widest range of reactions. My good friend Shira asked, "Whhhhhyyyy?" Her vocal inflection suggested slight concern and bemused confusion as to why anyone would choose this. Most, though, were highly encouraging: they often called me brave. I found that hard to hear—or to believe. Especially as I feel anything but brave at this time.

The best words of encouragement for this trip came from my eighty-five-year-old mother-in-law, Helene. A feisty, spirited woman who loved me from the day we met, Helene takes my cheekiness and tosses it back without a blink of an eye. She's a tiger and a kitten all in one. And she knows a thing or two about doing challenging walks. She took up hiking when she turned fifty and decided to hike in Nepal, near Everest. She also knew why I was hiking the Camino and all that was at stake.

Helene had only two words of advice: walk softly.

I WASN'T SURE WHAT WALKING SOFTLY WOULD LOOK LIKE, but as soon as she said it, I knew that was exactly what I needed to do. Just a few days earlier, facing forty staff members at the theatre where I am the artistic director, I burst into tears as I announced on a Zoom call that I needed to leave them for five weeks. I used the word "need" so they didn't think I was trying

to slip in a badly timed vacation. I had already decided it was best to come clean and tell everyone why I had to go.

In front of this mass of faces online, I began: "As you know, I'm going on a sabbatical. I will be away and out of reach for five weeks. I'll be hiking in Spain. What I haven't explained to you fully is that, for the past six months, my mental health has been . . ." I faltered and couldn't find the right words. "I'm not myself." I started to cry. Speaking through my tears, I laid it all out, true and honest. "I'm a mess, actually. And I hope that this time away will help me recharge . . . and make it possible for me to lead you once again."

It wasn't the stunned and uncomfortable faces staring back at me that were the most alarming. What shocked and scared me the most was looking at my fifty-three-year-old image on the screen. I barely recognized myself. My eyes were red and swollen. My face drooped into a desperate expression. I looked how I felt—lost and frightened.

"I need this time. I hope you'll understand."

Trying not to throw everyone into a panic, I added, "Don't worry, I will be back at the theatre next month. I won't be announcing my new career as a yoga teacher." Lisa, from wardrobe, shared a supportive laugh—always one of the first to be encouraging in any way she can. I was trying to seem confident, but in my heart I was doubting if I would return. Looking at the gallery of faces, I saw compassion and empathy but also deep discomfort. Most people were silent. Karen, from audience services, offered, "We want you to go, but please come back."

After the call, sitting alone in my office and wiping off my tears, the image of my on-screen self still haunting me, fear overcame me. Would I even be able to get on a plane by myself? Was that safe?

AS IT TURNED OUT, my worries weren't exaggerated. Just flying from Toronto to Spain was a marathon-level ordeal. There weren't any direct flights from Canada to Spain—they had all been suspended. Air routes around the world had been cut back, and COVID had sent all airlines into scheduling chaos. My original flight was routed through England, but that segment was cancelled only last week. The new, makeshift version took me on an absurd route—beginning with a quick two-hour flight west from Toronto to Chicago yesterday. For my layover, it was a painfully dull eight hours of walking up and down every corridor of O'Hare International Airport (though I did enjoy checking out a cute sailor all dressed in white). I couldn't leave the Chicago airport soon enough and was grateful to escape on an Iberia Airlines flight to Madrid. To add insult to my not-ideal travel planning, the plane flew back east—practically over my house in Canada—as if to say, "Well, that's ten hours you're never getting back. Happy hiking, loser."

I NEED COFFEE.

With extended, mouth-widening yawns, I walk with my backpack in search of a restaurant that might be open in this empty airport. I find a stylish café and approach the server hesitantly. I will attempt speaking Spanish, while half-awake. In the past, I've been that terrified tourist who can't eke out one phrase in another language without panicking. I've recently begun taking Spanish classes, so I'm committed to trying. And I was warned about the speed at which Spaniards speak. I experience this while ordering. I listen and scramble to grab on to one Spanish word from the waitress. That's what my Spanish teacher always told us: find the one verb—seize it, repeat it back, and add something basic to it, with a dash of kindness.

Señora: *"Hola! Buenos días. ¿Qué te gustaría beber?"*

"Gustaría" translates to "would like." *What would I like to drink? Got it.*

Dennis: *"Me gustaría un café con leche, por favor."*
I sip my aromatic, deliciously textured coffee.
I glance all around.
I soak in everything as silence surrounds me.
I breathe.

I think of the effort to make it here. I've escaped. After seventeen months since this pandemic began, I've found my way out.

Even getting to the airport yesterday morning was a massive challenge, as much as I desperately needed this trip. Whenever I travel, the minutes before I walk out of my house are always the worst. Thirty hours ago, at home back in Ontario, a surge of doubt had overwhelmed me, and what had seemed like a brilliant plan transformed into a stupid idea that should be abandoned before going to the airport. The cab was five minutes late, and I said to Bruce, my husband, "That's it—I'm going back to bed—the trip is off." (Well, it was four in the morning.)

I do have a flair for the dramatic.

It's even in my job description. I'm an artistic director of a theatre company. Or I was. Or I still am. Hopefully this pilgrimage will help me sort all this out.

I have been contemplating the first few days of the Camino, thought to be the hardest and yet most memorable part of the hike, for weeks now. I know the journey will include walking with other confused, tired, and lost souls. And I predict that, at some point, I will crave companionship. However, I'm committed to walking alone and in silence as much as possible, at least to begin with. I need to calm the noise in my head.

With my coffee long finished, I wander again up and down the empty airport. Two hours spent, four to go. I read every sign, step into every store knowing full well there is no room in my pack for anything more. I stroll and discover every corner of the complex. I buy my first sandwich made of Iberian ham.

Using my best pointing skills, I make it through the ordering process. The chewing keeps me awake.

Looking up between bites, I see a bookstore across the terminal. Ordinarily, I would want to check it out. The old me was always interested in discovering new fiction, especially novels that might be made into great adaptations for the stage. But now the closed bookstore with all its promising stories behind iron bars only reminds me of the relentless sinking weight in my chest and a particularly devastating day seventeen months ago.

OPENING NIGHT?

On the morning of every opening night at the theatre where I have been since 2016, the staff gathers for a celebratory breakfast. The Grand Theatre is in London, Ontario, Canada, and the building itself is a marvel. Built in 1901, the proscenium arch, adorned with a century-old hand-painted mural, makes it an architectural standout. Expansive at eight hundred seats, the theatre is still intimate enough for audiences to perceive the finest details; actors love to perform in this space where you can truly hear a pin drop in silent moments.

That night we were supposed to be opening the world-premiere stage version of the bestselling novel *Room*, written by the extraordinary Emma Donoghue. Many people know *Room* as an Academy Award–winning film starring Brie Larson. This internationally acclaimed novel about a woman locked in a room with her five-year-old son focuses on how she endures, escapes, and finds her way back into the world. It has been brilliantly imagined for the stage by Emma and the director Cora Bissett. Emma calls Canada home after immigrating from Ireland a couple of decades ago. She lives here in London, Ontario, a midsize city halfway between Toronto and Detroit. Emma has only a thirty-minute walk from her door to ours.

Room is a hard-hitting story: Ma has a child in captivity through abuse by a man who has locked her in a shed for many years. Ma's resilience helps her raise this kid to believe that the shed, this "room," is actually the world. Little Jack has no understanding that there is life outside the eleven-by-eleven-foot space. At the end of act 1, through Ma's brilliant resourcefulness, the boy escapes and Ma is discovered. Act 2 follows life for the two of them in the "world." And they discover that life outside has its own challenges. At the Grand, for three nights of public previews, our audiences were drawn in by Ma's resilience to make it out.

Our production had been two years in development, and after the curtain came down on the final preview, Cora turned to me, beaming, and said, "Now, we're ready to open." The little boy playing Jack, nine-year-old Quinsley, was confident, and the very tricky stage machinery was fully programmed to rotate the entire set, exposing all four sides of the room as if under a microscope. The cast was pitch-perfect.

The opening night was to be of great significance as well. The impressive and powerful Mirvish Productions had collaborated with us, as had Sam Julyan of Covent Garden Productions in the United Kingdom. Following the run at the Grand for a month, the production would transfer to the theatre district in Toronto. Being presented in Toronto, a major theatre city in the world, would give *Room* a shot at getting produced on larger stages, perhaps even in New York.

I consider opening nights to be a gift back to all involved, where we pause and acknowledge all the work that goes into a production. It's usually a day of great excitement. Some artists hate this day—it's too stressful (and the actors still have to perform and need to drown out the noisy excitement, to be true to what has been rehearsed). But for me, it is usually pure joy. I laugh. I applaud. I celebrate.

But by six in the morning, I was beginning to realize opening night may become closing night. The day before, the National Basketball Association eerily cancelled their entire season, and government announcements made it clear that COVID was making public gatherings unsafe.

At eight o'clock that morning, executive director Deb Harvey, my co-leader, and I gathered the six board executives for an emergency meeting by phone. We collectively agreed that, for the first time in my life, the show would not go on. The health of everyone was in jeopardy, and it would not be prudent for us to invite eight hundred people into our building that night. For two hours, Deb and I kept this secret while putting the emergency plan in place.

When the two of us arrived at the staff breakfast, the excitement for opening night was palpable. The staff didn't know what news was about to come their way. We let everyone get their food and eat for a few minutes. We thought they would need that. Deb and I stood up to speak. We looked out to a room of engaged and dedicated theatre people. In the past, we would begin breakfast with a toast. Not that day. "We have some terrible news," Deb began. "As you know, there is a virus going around the world, and because of that, we are not going to open the show tonight." Her voice broke, emotions overtook her, and she did something I have never seen her do before: she turned away, overcome.

A shot of adrenalin pulsed through me and I took over. "We are not opening *Room* tonight," I offered directly. "I am sorry to say that we are cancelling the entire performance run. We won't have the public in our building for the next two months."

As I said these words, I watched faces of joy turn into faces of sadness and fear and disbelief. Tears were running down people's cheeks as I started to lay out the details and logic. Hands were covering faces. Eyes were widening. I tried to keep it factual, with limited emotion.

"Any questions?" I asked quietly.

Silence.

Breakfast dissolved quickly as people walked away speechless. An entire building of theatre people moved around in shock—dazed, silent, and with eyes to the ground.

I called Emma. "I'm sorry to tell you we have to postpone the entire production. We won't be opening your beautiful show tonight."

"I understand. I hope you are alright," she said, her empathy for us her priority. "Stay well."

We spent the rest of that day calling people, cancelling projects, and contacting thousands of subscribers as well. We proceeded quickly, doing things that none of us had ever done before.

The creative team got on their flights back to the United Kingdom over the weekend, never having seen the completion of their project. What moved us forward that day was the belief that we would lose only the rest of our season—two months. We would bring the show back at a later date. The costs were unknown, but the likely lost revenue would be in the hundreds of thousands of dollars. Deb and I were clear and determined that it would have no impact on the following season, which we had recently announced only a week previous: fifteen productions and a national tour of our hit production of *Cabaret*—all costing us eight million dollars. But we were excited and confident about having a terrific playbill to celebrate our return. On top of all this, there was the planned renovation of our theatre, at a cost of nine million dollars, which was supposed to be squeezed into this summer when the theatre was closed. The future of the renovation became uncertain.

We told everyone over and over that day—Friday the thirteenth—that we would take the hit now so that we could be back to normal in two months.

SEVENTEEN MONTHS LATER

As I FINISH THE REMAINS OF MY FIRST SPANISH LUNCH, in the Madrid airport, I try not to contemplate the failed opening night of *Room* and all that came after. But my mind keeps taking me there. I have to admit it to myself: the last seventeen months have been absolute hell. We haven't produced any theatre; in addition to *Room*, all the productions that were supposed to have followed were cancelled. The renovation is in process—moving slowly with COVID safety restrictions and construction shortages dominating the effort. The stress of keeping the company from going into huge debt combined with keeping staff employed is a constant pressure that hasn't let up since that devastating opening night. Sitting in the surreal stillness of what should be a bustling international airport, I can't help but think about the many artistic leaders around the world who have been able to cope with all the turmoil COVID has caused. Not me.

I don't feel prepared, and yet I've never felt more ready for a solo pilgrimage.

After passing a sea of empty departing gates where airplanes and passengers should be crowding around, I hand my boarding pass to the gate attendant and find my seat on a plane with only a handful of passengers. By sheer will or sheer exhaustion, I manage to push away the fears about my fragile mental state and whether any of this is a good idea, and somehow lull myself into a brief, fitful sleep.

A few hours later, after landing in northern Spain at San Sebastián Airport in the town of Irún, I walk out the modest airport's sliding doors and head on foot directly to the pension where I'm staying for the night. It's a bit of a shock to discover that my first steps are in an ugly urban blight. Here in Irún, mildly unimportant older buildings crumble as they sit too close to the busy roads—as if the city planners didn't even notice the buildings were there in the first place. I'm not sure if Irún has even had better days. It's a brutal introduction to a land I have dreamed of visiting for a long time.

As I head toward my hotel, having studied and practiced this short route to the pension online many times back in Canada, I start to realize that my scale is off, and I can't figure out where the train station is. I'm not relying on any technology—or even an old-fashioned map—as I assumed this would be easy enough to find on its own. The pension is one street over from the train station, so if I can find the station, I can find the pension. How difficult could it be to find a train station in a European city? However, I'm a tad bit lost mere minutes into my journey. Not good. That's when the first miracle of my journey occurs: I ask a stranger for directions, using my limited Spanish.

I never ask for guidance when I'm lost. Never. I'm too shy, too proud, and too nervous to offend another human with a question. I'm the one in control—the director after all. Most times I would rather wander for hours than admit defeat and ask for help. And certainly not in a country where I don't speak the language. But I need to get to that pension. Summoning my newfound linguistic courage, I gesture to the first person who walks by: a leathery-skinned old man. With my vocabulary ready, I point in a direction and find the courage to speak:

"*¿Tren?*"

"*¿La estación de tren?*" would have been better. Or, "*Señor, pregunta: ¿Dónde está la estación de tren?*" He pauses, looks confused, and then responds quietly with a hundred words and thirty sentences. I respond with all I have at the moment:

"*¿Tren?*"

The old man begins speaking very quickly. This time gestures are added. I think he understands me. We are having a conversation now. He tells me something about where I need to go—that way, a few blocks, to the left. I'm understanding him! I start to walk in the direction indicated, and he follows alongside me. He carries on talking. This makes me nervous, as I've still contributed only one word (twice) to the conversation, but we are "speaking." Now the elderly gentleman is starting to clarify something, and numbers are added to the conversation. I begin to wonder if he is trying to swindle me—offer me something—trick me. And that's when miracle number two happens: my limited Spanish lessons kick in, and I finally understand what he is attempting to communicate.

"*¿Quieres tomar el tren de las seis y cuarto?*" he asks me.

I put together that the six-fifteen train to San Sebastián is leaving shortly and I had better move quickly if I want to catch it. I laugh with the pure joy of understanding, as I appreciate his concern. With confidence growing, I speak a few more words and explain to him that I'm actually looking for my hotel: "*Pension Bowling,*" I tell him. "*Cerca de la estación*" (Near the station). He nods with new understanding. More hand signals point me to turn right and then left and I will be there. "*Gracias.*" I walk ahead alone now, and when I'm close to where I think I should be, I slowly turn back, with the hope that this man is still watching me. I find comfort in his assistance. His eyes are still on me, and he begins waving now—I'm very close! At this moment I'm deeply grateful for this Spanish gentleman who doesn't judge me for my limitations but simply guides me on my way.

And I arrive, after going slightly off course, exactly where I need to be.

DINNER IN FRANCE

THE CAMINO DEL NORTE walking route officially begins on the border between France and Spain. More specifically, it begins on a bridge. It's a short walk to the bridge that spans the river in Irún, and many pilgrims skip the backtracking since the starting point is more symbolic than required. However, the chance to visit France for a couple of hours seems irresistible. After settling into the run-down pension, I walk two kilometres to France, carrying both my Canadian passport and my Camino passport, just in case.

On the bridge between Irún and the French city Hendaye, the border patrol stands guard. That is, there is a plastic patio shelter that looks like it would be more fitting in a backyard with a picnic table underneath. The guards stop cars randomly, but they don't take notice of people crossing the bridge on foot. My Canadian passport is not required here. However, I think it's cleverly planned that the first building I encounter on the French side is a brasserie and patisserie. *C'est magnifique!*

Heading for the tourist information office, I spot a rather elegant woman in the booth who might assist in giving me my very first "passport stamp" on my Camino journey. To confirm my commitment to the Camino, I can optionally participate in obtaining stamps in a booklet, officially called the *credencial del peregrino*. Locals standing by with the stamps for the Camino pilgrim passport can be found in hotels, churches, bars, or in this case a French information booth. I had brought along my Camino passport in hopes I might find someone who could ceremoniously give me my first stamp. It is an incredibly exciting moment for me. The woman behind the desk continues speaking on the phone throughout our exchange. She opens an ink pad, reaches for a stamp, warms the stamp with the red ink, and lifts it through the air to my awaiting pilgrim passport. She presses the rubber onto the paper, never once looking up at me, and continues speaking rapidly to a person on the other end of the phone without pausing. Regardless, I'm beaming.

It's official: I have begun my Camino.

Across from the information office, I sit on the patio of the charming brasserie I first passed at the border. While watching the traffic going by and soaking in a little French culture, I enjoy my *entrecôte* steak *frites* with a lovely glass of wine from Burgundy. Delicious. Any attempts at speaking French are short-circuited by my recent stockpiling of useful Spanish words into my brain. My responses, in other words, are atrocious. Being from Canada, where French and English are both our official languages, I should be able to do better. My mother, Huguette, was born and raised in the province of Quebec and spoke both languages fluently. I never learned French. The tall and dark, sultry waitress who is serving me is from Russia. She tells me she speaks French, Spanish, English, and Russian. I don't have my vaccine passport on me (so many passports to carry!), and in France it is required for dining. That passport is tucked inside my knapsack back at the hotel. She shouldn't serve me while I'm sitting on the patio, but she does. She's frustrated by the rules and tells me the police do random checks on her restaurant weekly and are aggressive in their interrogation. She finds it exhausting—she just wants to serve people. When I explain that I'm about to walk the Camino, the waitress admits she's heard of it but is too busy working to find the time to walk it. *"Bon voyage,"* she offers, with the warmest smile.

As I cross back on the bridge, walking across the invisible line that we call a border, I feel a sense of relief that I have made it this far.

And I have had French wine in France.

It is August 11, 2021, and I am ready to begin.

I think.

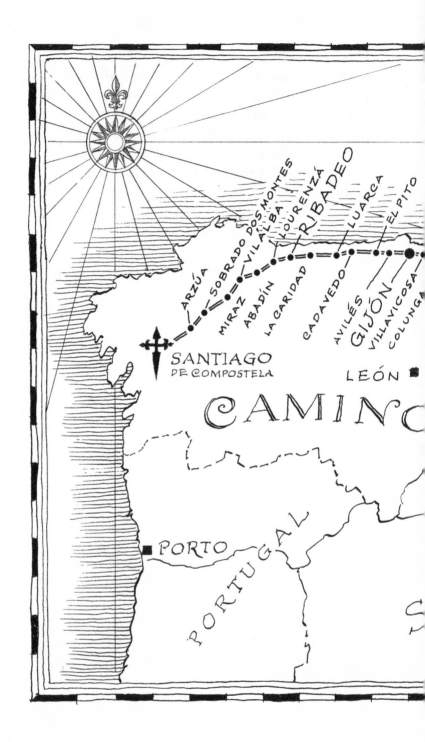

WEEK ONE

THE JOY OF SOLITUDE

There are seven official Catholic Camino routes—and all lead to a particular gothic cathedral in the heart of the city known as Santiago in northwestern Spain. They are a holy pilgrimage of incredible distance, requiring the stamina to walk over eight hundred kilometres. Of these seven Caminos, the most famous path is called the Camino Francés. Approximately 180,000 people walk this route annually. A decade ago, Hollywood made a movie about this particular Camino, *The Way*, and the crowds have been coming in record numbers ever since. It's considered the one to walk first: difficult, but not impossible, and full of amenities along the way. However, there are alternatives. The Camino del Norte caught my interest and attention very quickly when I poured over options. The del Norte mostly hugs the Atlantic coastline, and sometimes even tracks the hiker directly across its stunning beaches. It's far less popular, as it's considered the most challenging due to the intensity of the topography. Often the path plummets toward the ocean and then climbs straight back up. Fewer than twenty thousand people walk the del Norte in a given year, just over 10 percent of the walkers on the Camino

Francés. These aspects made it all the more appealing to me. I wanted the challenge and the quiet of the north.

COVID is ravaging the world, and recently Spain has moved to a higher level of alert: "RED." I'm comforted that I will spend most of my time outdoors and spaced far from other humans. Masks are required indoors and, where it is crowded, in public squares. I'm hopeful I will keep safe and not get sick. I will be vigilant.

In all the guidebooks (I cross-referenced most of them), this first day starting in Irún is considered a highlight of the entire Camino del Norte. It's a strenuous hike upward, along ridges, with stunning ocean views on offer. It's a challenge hikers live for. Walking for twenty-five kilometres to the seaside town of San Sebastián will centre me clearly in Spain today. I didn't sleep well last night, as I checked my watch every few hours. *Can I start yet? Is it time?* As I look out the tiny window of my shabby room when I rise this morning, my heart sinks. On what should have been a gloriously warm and sunny summer day, I see nothing but extensive clouds filling the sky, some so low they obscure the tops of the mountains I'm about to climb. There is rain in those clouds. Forget the ocean views; I will be walking among the clouds with little chance of seeing the ocean below. I laugh to myself. So much for today going as planned. Was I asking too much? How did I ever think it would go smoothly? Why should today be any different than the last five hundred days?

Packing my knapsack requires some serious concentration this morning. The brand name (Gregory) of the pack is stitched in white capital letters below the logo with two mountains. I've yet to carry this pack on a single hike. It feels too impersonal to not be on a first-name basis, given what we are about to share, so I've decided to call my backpack Gregory from now on.

The first things I place in Gregory are my life essentials:

one change of non-hiking clothes (must have a collared shirt for the evenings, to relieve my hiking shirt), compact toiletries (it's tricky finding a tiny deodorant), a detailed map-filled guidebook (my lifeline), and a pair of collapsible hiking poles. And then there is a different kind of life-essential item—a small, humble rock.

As I waited for the cab at four in the morning in my house in Canada, Bruce presented it to me—sitting like a statue in his palm. "Will you take this with you?" he asked.

I smiled. "To remember you and Abby?" I asked. We have an eleven-year-old daughter.

He smiled. "Yes. It's from us. Pilgrims are supposed to bring a rock from their homeland. This one's from the west coast, where we were hiking last month. Place all your burdens, challenges, and problems into the rock. And then, when you are ready, leave it somewhere on the path. You'll know when's best."

"Brilliant idea. I'd love to leave my problems there," I said. "Thanks, honey. I love a mission."

I study the smooth rock in my palm and think of Bruce and Abby, and how hard it's been for them too. As bad as I've had it, I have to admit that my woes can't compare to being a middle schooler shut at home with her parents day in and day out. My thoughts go to Bruce and how he is supporting both of us now—using every ounce of optimism he has. The weight of the rock begins to feel reassuring, a holder of all that I might want to leave behind in Spain.

"Bienvenido a España, rock."

As I place each item into Gregory, I pause and give stern looks at a couple that aren't exactly life essentials—a small paperback novel, an extra water bottle—fully judging them for their value and wondering why I have included them. At this point every item added is another item of weight. However, I'm not willing to leave anything behind yet. I've put too much planning, list making, and organizing into this to start doubting the contents of my pack. Not wise on the morning of day one to be tossing things away, I tell myself. But let this be a word of warning to the dearest items that Gregory is holding: prove your worth, or you will be left behind. I head out of my pension exactly thirty minutes later this morning than I had told myself I would. I'll do better tomorrow.

Now with my sense of direction intact, I head back through town. I calculate five hours of walking today. I feel fresh and ready to take on that challenge. My love of this city isn't improving—it's a bit of a sprawling mess with little sense of cohesion. But, for now, my only concern is to follow any yellow arrow or painted scalloped shell. These two symbols are the universal "go this way" markers for pilgrims hiking any of the traditional Camino routes. Lose sight of these and I will lose sight of my goal. Fortunately, it seems that no surface is off-limits when it comes to these arrows. Official posts in the ground are welcomed, but so are yellow arrows painted on trees, sidewalks, sides of buildings, and any place available. These arrows will be my lifeline for my entire adventure.

After a few minutes, the hike is routed beside a stream in a very old part of town. The terrain becomes hilly, and the views start to become, dare I say, beautiful. My jaw drops—I'm shocked to see such pastoral loveliness in this town I have basically written off. The buildings are now century-old cottages, and I'm walking on ancient dirt roads. Dogs and chickens roam free. The air smells fresher, and the farmland is bountiful. I ascend toward the Santuario de Guadalupe church: higher and higher and everything starts to morph into a different perspective. The views of the city below, the countryside, and even the detail in the cloudy skies open up. In what feels like mere moments, I'm walking in bucolic, serene solitude and it is bliss.

I take in the surroundings.

I take in the silence.

I take a deep breath.

Bruce once explained to me his idea of the difference between an extrovert and an introvert. Extroverts get their energy from other people. Introverts receive their energy from themselves. While Bruce is a model case study in extroversion (he loves to be surrounded by people and to help them), my introverted self gets great pleasure in being alone in my own solitude. When my introversion is charged up, I am good to go. Here on this cliff, I have this feeling that I've been so distracted trying to understand the troubles of others that I've lost all connection with myself, which is probably what contributed to the crisis I find myself in. This solitude feels long overdue and is deeply welcome medicine. My introverted self is smiling.

As I breathe in this air, my spirits start to lift, my chest expands. It's been a long time since I've been in such alluring surroundings. It feels hopeful. I've missed this kind of immersion profoundly. I walk to a large stone protruding on the side of the road. From here I can see over the town and down to the ocean. I close my eyes, listen to the sound of my breathing, and remind myself to be present in every moment I can.

I begin to walk softly.

Up high on the mountain, I arrive at the first church of many to come, and the view from the grounds of this *santuario* is outstanding. Tour groups of chatty cyclists are congregating. Day hikers are resting and drinking their water for rejuvenation. I step inside the dark church, move to a pew in the back, and kneel. I'm thinking of my lovely mom, who passed away eight years ago. In her eighty-one years of life, she never missed going to mass every week. She was a devout Catholic. Mom would have loved that I'm on this journey, stopping at churches along the way. She would want me to stop in and say a prayer.

Growing up Catholic was a complicated experience, however. In my twenties, when I came out as a gay man, I eventually renounced my religion. I began to call myself a "former Catholic," since the rules were very clear: homosexuals were not welcome. So the great complication of this hike—of the many hikes I could have chosen in the world—is that, created over a thousand years ago, it exists primarily for Catholics. I know non-Catholics walk it, but they also don't have the fifty-plus years of baggage and knowledge of the meanings, rituals, and expectations that I do. As I throw myself forward, I am also propelling myself back.

In my pack, I've brought two letters that are over twenty years old each. I haven't looked at them in all these years, but I've included them in hopes they will clarify some unspoken feelings I have about leaving the Catholic Church years ago. I'll open them when it feels right. Not yet though, not yet. It feels too soon, in this church, to open those letters. I rise from the pew, genuflect, perform the sign of the cross, and walk back into the morning light.

Now that I'm a seasoned Camino hiker (ninety minutes into my walk makes it so), I carry on to a high-level route with expansive views of the sweeping ocean—well, they would be if the clouds weren't so low. I pull myself up a steep muddy ascent that goes on for a very long time, and I continue along a glorious path, looking to my right and imagining that I'm seeing the Atlantic Ocean. What I do savour is this sense of isolation, and the fact that I have made it here on my own. My plan is working.

Day hikers are on the mountain today. Most of them are stupidly fit, young, and good looking. Some of them are running up here, following the mountaintop, bouncing along as if this were an easy walk in the park. I'm in good company. Does that mean I am fitter than I think I am? My speedily-thrown-together training program consisted of many days of city walking back home. My longest day was four hours; I could have walked longer, but, frankly, it just got boring toddling down city streets. I eventually added Gregory to my training regime. Walking with a loaded backpack was intended to prepare me for this eventual reality. I noticed while training that cars stopped more swiftly and pedestrians gave me extra room. The look on people's faces was precious, as if they wanted to say, *Where are you from, and why in the hell would you walk through downtown with a backpack on?* If only they knew that, in order to simulate the prospective weight, I filled it with the only heavy things I could find: six bottles of dry white wine from the Niagara region.

I NOTICE SOMEONE UP ahead who might be a pilgrim.

This is the first fellow hiker whom I've come across—the size of the backpack makes it clear. So far this morning I've been free of committed Camino walkers. I start to slow down. I don't want to say hello to the person. And I find it awkward: Do I have to say hello just because we are doing the same thing? Can I just walk, head down, in silence? Solitude is my plan today—*please, world, let something go the way I'd like.* It's been too many months of plans being created, plans started, and plans postponed indefinitely. I don't think I can pivot one more time. Let this day just go as planned. *Hikers stay away from me!*

I keep slowing my pace, trying to avoid contact. I pause. Pretend to check a map. Look at the skies. Anything to create distance. Eventually I carry on, thinking I've put plenty of space between myself and that walker by now. As I scramble around a rather hefty boulder, the dreaded pilgrim pokes her face out from the other side. I'm trapped. This woman with adorably curly and bouncy hair smiles brightly and, in a clear British accent filled with warmth, says, "Good morning—I didn't see you there." I smile. I exchange greetings. I keep moving, awkwardly propelling my way forward and feeling rather rude not to engage.

But today is a solo day.

That's the plan.

I walk on.

Twenty minutes later, I'm confused about the direction I should be going. The obscuring clouds are making the orientation of everything a bit trickier to navigate. It looks like I'm walking through marshmallows. And a wrong turn could mean I end up walking back to Irún by mistake. My sense of direction is in question. Am I turned around? Am I backtracking? Out of necessity, not desire, I approach the British woman, who has appeared again. "Excuse me, do you think we are lost?" I ask, feebly.

"No." Her brow knits as she scans the landscape quickly. "Why do you think that?"

"I'm just worried we are headed backward. Where's the ocean?"

She smiles and points downward into the low-level clouds. "There, I think." We laugh.

She pulls out her phone. She has a GPS app that is tracking her every move. "We're headed in the right direction. If San Sebastián is your goal, that is."

"Yes, it is." Drat. We are going the same way. An awkward interaction commences. In my mind, I'm back at my high school dance at Catholic Central, shuffling with a girl across the dance floor, pretending to be interested. Here on the Camino, this woman walks a bit forward, I walk a bit forward; I point and awkwardly say, "Bird." She nods. We shuffle some more. She describes a flower clinging to the side of the cliff. I nod, feigning interest.

"Where are you from?"

"Canada. You?"

"I live in Switzerland now, but I'm from England."

We're talking in longer sentences, and I fear this means that we are now technically walking together. Is this how that happens? Are we dating? It never ended well at the school dances. Should I make a run for it?

After about an hour of walking and chatting together, I silently decide to give up my solitude for today and to embrace what is unfolding before me. After all, she is my favourite species: "British female." I have the biggest soft spot for British women. It's the accent, the dignity, the style, the poise. It goes back to Juliet Stevenson, with whom I fell wildly in love while watching her pour her guts out in the movie *Truly, Madly, Deeply*. And that damn Judi Dench! A brilliant stage actor whom I'd pay a million bucks to have dinner with. *Judi, do you love doing the Bond movies? Is Daniel Craig that sexy up close? And what do you think: shall I direct you in a play at the Grand Theatre?*

But I digress.

It turns out that this British woman has a compelling story of her own to tell. Within the first hour, she shares with me that this is her third time walking the Camino. She speaks openly. Her husband had been cheating on her for ten years, gave her short notice that her marriage was over, and walked out. It left her completely lost. She hit rock bottom. Three years ago, broken, she walked the Camino alone. "It saved my life," she says gently. I'm taken aback that my first conversation with a fellow walker goes directly to this level of openness so rapidly and easily.

Now, she tells me lightly, she is set up comfortably for life, thanks to a very large divorce settlement. She is free to hike for months at a time. She is saucy, kind, and warm. And her name is Joy. How perfectly apt.

Our day is spent sharing stories. I call my reason for being here "burnout" and leave it at that. It's accurate enough, but certainly not complete. Joy schools me in the Camino way, being deeply experienced in this road we are travelling. At her insistence, we take off our socks and shoes at lunchtime in the small riverside village of San Juan, while eating a warm chicken sandwich made by an elderly woman who sells food from the front room of her house.

After crossing the busy river in an oversize canoe-shaped boat, which takes under two minutes and costs seventy-five cents, we head toward the seaside city of San Sebastián. It begins to rain in the forest, and we rush to cover up by pulling out our rain ponchos. I now learn an important Camino lesson: always pack your raincoat to be accessible (next time, mine won't be stuck at the bottom of Gregory). San Sebastián looks like a mirage on approach: from up high and looking downward at a distance, hundreds of people are on the sandy, generously sized beach, celebrating their happy lives—living their dream under a cloud-filled sky. It's overcast, but that doesn't deter people from lazing about in the warmth of the day. The contrast with the dirtiness of Irún this morning is striking.

As we walk into the centre of town, I surprise myself. Solitude among all this humanity doesn't seem right, and the chance to share the city with my new friend seems necessary. I invite Joy to dinner.

"Joy, do you want to explore the old town with me tonight? I want to check out *pintxos*. That's what they call *tapas* here in Basque country. Meet on this corner at seven?"

There is a pause, and I wonder if I'm about to be turned down. Memories of the high school dance rejections flood back. "Yes. I'd love that. I'll see you tonight, thanks," Joy replies.

OLD TOWN IS BUSTLING with life as we scramble to find a free table at any restaurant that will have us. Luck is on our side, and a table for two just outside a front door becomes available after we wander the cobblestoned streets for a while. We dig into our *pintxos*—a lovely assortment of small offerings: shrimp on baguette, *tortilla de patatas*, stuffed peppers, croquettes. I open up more with Joy about my life—but not too much. It feels awkward and slightly painful to speak. I don't want to get pulled back to Canada and the somewhat terrifying, unresolved meltdown I experienced there. I want to be here and only here, in Spain. I'm just so happy to be laughing and talking about positive things. We hug as we say good night and promise to try to stay in touch, knowing that we may not see each other again, depending on our hiking rhythm.

The clouds never cleared on this first day. And what I thought would take five hours of walking took eleven gruelling hours. There was very little solitude to be had. It didn't go as planned at all.

It was glorious.

And on top of it all, I experienced Joy.

LOVESTRUCK

I FELL IN LOVE TODAY.

His name is Sebastián. Full name is San Sebastián. He's a beach town in northeastern Spain, renowned for many delectable things, including a large collection of Michelin three-star restaurants and a dramatic oceanfront featuring powerful waves crashing onto an expansive beach, making it ideal for surfing. This is complemented by a deeply sexy nightlife with the patrons of local bars spilling into the streets. All of it is filled with well-coiffed and gorgeously shaped people who spend their time strolling the seaside promenade with an understated grace. The architecture is both historically detailed and modernly sleek. No one is rushing; however, everyone is alive.

I love Sebastián and I can't stop thinking of him.

It wasn't in the original plans to have a rest day after one day of hiking. Who does that? The reason I am having a free day is rather accidental—however, I have decided, justified. When the airline changed my flight, the only way I could keep the rest of the schedule that I had meticulously planned was to leave one day early. It was an unorthodox decision that allowed me a free day at the start of this journey. The coin toss was to add an extra day in Irún or San Sebastián. Thank goodness. I won that flip of a coin.

I feel a bit like a Camino cheater today—knowing that Joy is walking ahead and I'm sleeping in, luxuriating in a small but stylish all-white hotel room. I get over my guilt thirty seconds after I step outside my hotel's front door and am exposed to the lively streets of this dazzling city. I spend the long afternoon on the beach watching surfers do what surfers do best: look impressive, act very serious and deeply focused, and crash and tumble into the waves frequently. They do it deftly. My brain is delightfully distracted by the sensations around me.

I book a massage and "me time" at La Perla spa. It's one of the most recognized tourist institutions here—not exactly off the beaten path. I'm far from being worthy of this after one day of hiking. A surge of my "Catholic guilt" concerning worthiness kicks in. However, I think a bit of relaxation and some time soaking in a pool would beautifully put the "rest" in "rest day." *Bruce would want me to not feel the guilt of this excess,* I tell myself. When in Spain . . .

At La Perla I'm introduced to an entirely different luxury experience that includes five pools, two hot and three cold; Jacuzzis; and a steam room with direct access to the sandy beach and the ocean. But the experience that truly delights me is the stand-up Jacuzzi. It's built within a larger pool, and when I arrive at the bubbly mess, I discover metal handles under the water awaiting my grasp. If I don't hold on, I will get swept away. I grab on and pull myself straight into the centre of the metal ring, not sure what to expect next. I'm surprised to feel water shooting straight up from below. I hold on as strongly as I can, and the sensation of the rushing water is euphoric. "This is incredible!" comes out of my mouth audibly. My inside voice cannot resist. "Woooooooooow!" I scream out. Luckily, the roaring sound of the water drowns out my enthusiastic words. No one takes notice. I'm beaming. This is the first time I have been inside a place like this since the pandemic started. My gym membership was the first thing I cancelled when the world began to shut down. Here, people are keeping their distance, and the doors and windows are all propped open. But I'm in these pools with other humans nearby. And it tilts into the feeling of normalcy.

Back on my stroll through the streets, I conclude that my boy Sebastián has many traits I haven't seen in other oceanside cities. He combines a natural circular beach area and harbour with thoughtfully designed, unimposing Belle Epoque architecture, fairy-tale palaces, and white puffy clouds gently bringing them quietly together. Perfection. It would make an excellent backdrop to a theatre set—maybe a romantic comedy where long-lost lovers meet and rekindle their passion for each other. They kiss and burst into song as the sun sets, with this gorgeous scenery acting as their background. . . .

There are some staggeringly sized churches, alleyways filled with artists busily creating in their studios, and the sounds of lives being lived pouring out of second- and third-floor apartment windows. Markets are filled with the colours of freshness: vibrant bright-purple flowers, just-caught red and shiny seafood, and black, white, and yellow root vegetables still covered in dirt. Sebastián doesn't feel overly snobbish or flashy or expensive, and yet there is style everywhere within him. It feels neither exclusive nor overly touristy and trod upon. It just feels right.

Older women here dress better than anyone I have ever seen. If you are over sixty here, you are leading the way. And if you are over seventy, watch out! I think one woman invented a nice shade of green just for her coat. And I hate green. How anyone gets away with a two-piece suit made of the same busy patterned fabric is beyond me. But get away with it they do.

As I stroll through the harbour at night alone, with the

sun setting over family gatherings, people dining, children playing, and fishing boats returning with the day's catch, I'm comforted by the calmness of it all. Humanity abounds here— Sebastián feels alive within the world and as its own world simultaneously. All is right with all the worlds, this city seems to be singing. I haven't seen beauty in this form for such a long time. And more significantly, I haven't let myself be inspired to even dream up a theatre backdrop for an even longer time. But it seems that my imagination is here visiting for the day—and reminding me of what was. I soak it in.

Thank you, my dear Sebastián. I won't forget you.

HANGIN' WITH SURFERS

TODAY I'M COMMITTED TO FINDING THE SOLITUDE I've been yearning for. Second time's the charm?

The path is delightfully empty and, at the start of the day, misty and cloudy. I'm still a novice at hiking this route, and now clearly on my own. I don't see anyone for a couple of hours. I am headed to Zarautz, also along the ocean. But to get there, I will walk inland past and through farmers' fields and dirt roads. I keep a lookout for the yellow arrows as my guideposts. Today is not as difficult as the walk to San Sebastián but still rugged and challenging at moments, full of ups and downs. Common sights on my hike include energetic horses, braying donkeys, lazy cows, noisy chickens, charming dogs, and sleepy sheep. Mixed among them is the pop-up collection of very cool humans congregating with their nomadic camper vans. They seem to find each other in parking lots scattered throughout the coast. No two vans are alike—personality and originality are key. There seems to be a subculture existing here. They're gathering behind their vans with their camping chairs and coolers. Surfboards are propped against open trailers—ready for action. Wet clothes are draped off the vans' back doors.

Could I be living out of a van one day? Maybe that's what the Camino is trying to teach me. *A bit of a stretch,* I think.

On the Camino I draw near the city of Zarautz from the most incredible vantage point: I approach the edge of a monumental mountaintop looking down at one of the largest beaches in Europe. It seems to go on forever. There must be at least three thousand people playing down below, with room enough to be "socially distanced"—a phrase that has emerged during this pandemic. After I descend two hundred steep concrete stairs built perfectly into the hillside, I arrive at a boardwalk with extensive netting attached. It's an unexplainable detail until I notice the golf course on the other side of the boardwalk. I'm now greatly appreciative of being protected inside all this netting as I walk.

Regularly on the Camino there are a series of municipal *albergues* that have bunk beds for pilgrims such as myself. Access is by donation. You can pay as little as ten euros for a bed. It's a very comfortable option and a way to have pilgrims meet (am I a pilgrim yet?). No advance booking is required, but they usually fill up, so people have to come early enough to avoid a full house. However, due to COVID, most of these gathering places are shut down—the idea of communal living being quite the opposite of a safe measure during this time. It makes my journey more expensive and requires some extra planning and foresight. More-commercial accommodations, such as hotels and hostels, will be my mainstay.

It's the middle of August now—high season in this surfer town, so there are very few options for me to consider. The *albergue* is closed, and the hotels are incredibly pricey. Therefore I sign up for the "surfers' hostel"—big mistake right there. When I'm shown to my tiny bunk, I have a sense of doom. I'm not in the right place. This is not me. The tight lobby is filled with very cool kids in their twenties, and I truly have never felt older than I do today. To make matters worse, near midnight

I turn into "that old man" who has to ask two young women not to giggle in their bunks. I suggest that maybe they could go to the lobby if they want to keep their conversation going. They respond immediately and graciously, which only makes me think I'm a super-ancient, old fuddy-duddy. That night the surfers, bikers, and I are "sleeping" together in a room not friendly to COVID precautions—all of us in our little capsules. I can't sleep more than ten minutes at a time—between the choruses of snores, movement, and general upheaval. I rise very early in the morning, while most in my crowded room (including those two women) sleep soundly. I am happy for them that, when they awaken, they'll be able to say, "Thank God that old fella's gone."

Sometimes it is about pushing your boundaries, and sometimes it is about finding your people. I won't miss the surfers' hostel. When we hike, Bruce and I talk about how day one is usually "adrenaline awesome," how day two can become "cancel this nightmare," and how day three becomes "the best thing ever." Yesterday wasn't outright painful, but it did make me think there is a long road ahead.

Onward to day three.

PERCHANCE

I ESCAPE FROM THE SURFERS' HOSTEL in the dark of morning, with only streetlamps lighting my way. The first hour is spent hiking directly along the ocean's edge—a paved road clinging to the mountainside. Mist fills the air as I take in the solitude that has returned; I hear only the sound of waves hitting the shore. As I walk this route, I spot sporting officials and police officers setting up for an event: a marathon. Notices indicate that this seaside path will be shut down in a few hours to make way for official runners. I feel true elation to be here just before the runners begin and also relief that I'm getting ahead of them before this road is locked down. I silently wish them success.

As I hike through all the excitement loaded down with Gregory, I notice that no one is judging me or my hiking costume: no lingering stares to suggest, *What are you doing with that large backpack on?* Or, *You call yourself a hiker? Walking alone?* I'm blending in. Or more appropriately, I'm feeling less like a fake. I think I can consider myself a genuine hiker.

And it wasn't always this way.

Two decades ago, a couple of hours meandering through downtown in my running shoes was a big, exhausting adventure for me. I can pinpoint the moment that I crossed over to an adventurous outdoor lifestyle. And I can point my finger at the person who taught me, inspired me, and challenged me to do this: Bruce.

When we met, Bruce had already experienced much adventurous travelling: hiking through New Zealand, a solo time with Outward Bound in Utah, backpacking through Europe—it was in his bones. The winter we met, in 2000, Bruce wanted to rent a cottage with me for a week during the upcoming summer. I was in my early thirties, and all I had ever known was a busy life. There are no such things as weekends in the theatre—we just work. The idea that we would go away and cut off from the world for a week was a nightmarish thought. I reluctantly agreed to follow his lead after much protesting, begging, challenging, and doubting that me in the wilderness was something anyone needed to be a part of. But he's a determined one and used all his charm to make my no become a yes. For me, a week at a cottage was a week wasted. However, it was early dating days, and I was trying to be on my best behaviour.

Bruce found us a cottage in Algonquin Park, one of Ontario's most majestic and preserved areas. Any cottage building and further ownership were stopped by the Canadian government in the 1950s in order to preserve and protect the land. The government did allow any existing buildings to remain. However, all properties were frozen in time: only small electric motorboats are allowed, and no hydro-electric power can be installed. The cottage Bruce rented from an American family had gas lamps and a propane fridge. Limited at best. No power, no indoor plumbing, and we would have to transfer by boat to reach it.

It sounded like pure hell to me.

With my fear of drowning in large bodies of water on overdrive, I put on my life jacket twenty minutes before our water taxi arrived. I boarded the small boat, confident that it would capsize and I would drown. However, as the boat meandered gently down seldom experienced waterways, my heart started to open. When the boat turned a bend in the water, in the distance I saw our place for the next week sitting among the trees: preserved in time, humble in scale, and so incredibly inviting—a true Canadian cottage.

Outside of a theatre, it was the most beautiful thing I had ever seen in my life.

I started to breathe in a way I never knew was possible.

Deeply.

Effortlessly.

During that week I took off all my clothes, jumped in the water, and swam naked for the very first time. It was a baptism in freedom. I would race to the outhouse while listening carefully for any approaching bears. And Bruce taught me to stern a canoe through some of Algonquin Park's most inviting watery landscapes, always on the lookout for a moose. This sort of exertion was new to me and would become invaluable in my future life as a hiker.

And for the first time in my entire life, I was living in the moment.

Up until then, I had always been on the move to the next thing—always planning the future event. During this cottage week, I focused on the meal in front of me, not the meal that would be cooked later at dinner. This was an entirely new experience for me. I was breathing and thinking and living in the present. I stopped to smell the proverbial roses. I loved every second of it, spending most of the week in the lake without a swimsuit. The time flew by in an instant, but I was forever changed. And I grew to admire Bruce in a whole new way.

A few months later, on my thirty-third birthday, I cleverly

suggested to Bruce that we look at buying a cottage—"just for fun," I said. Over a fall weekend, with leaves turning to bright yellows, reds, and oranges, we looked at ten different cottages of various sizes, from mansions to shacks. We walked into a little A-frame cottage that was seven hundred square feet. Bob, the impressively experienced real estate agent, said to us, "You won't like it, it's too small." He was wrong. My imagination could see beyond what it was to what it could be. It had a full view of the lake, a dock, and a firepit, and most importantly, it had the potential to be our own unique rustic escape. My creative cells were firing with ideas.

Bruce and I had only been dating for six months and lived in two different rental apartments. But somehow I had tricked him (or had he tricked me?). I used all the money I had saved in my life for my half of the deposit. Thankfully, due to its size, it was inexpensive. We named the cottage Perchance, as in "perchance to dream" from Shakespeare, because that's how it came to us—by chance. One of my good friends, Allan, who also had taught me theatre design at university, subsequently designed us a little guesthouse on the water's edge; all the walls slide open so that sleeping in this screened-in mini-barn is a summer highlight for all who visit. Twenty years later, Perchance is still our favourite place on the planet and continues to inspire us.

AFTER SEEING MY HEART AND CONFIDENCE OPENING UP during that first cottage week, Bruce started challenging the notion of what holidays could be for us.

We were invited to a wedding in Europe a few years later. Our two stylish friends Alex and Charlie were to be wed on a family yacht moored in the Monaco harbour. The SS *Delphine* was a recently refurbished luxury yacht from the 1930s. To round out this impossibly dreamy offer, we began the holiday with an extended multi-day hike. This was the first time I would hike for more than one day. Using a private local travel company to plan it all for us, we walked across the French island of Corsica. The company charted a route from town to town, organized our bag transfers, and booked our hotels. We hiked together—just the two of us. The company sorted out all the logistics. It was a one-hundred-kilometre hike across the island. The convenience of the bag transfers and hotels made it an easier first step for me. We were hiking in September, when the weather consisted of warm days and cool nights. I wasn't convinced I could make it through, at the start—I was quite nervous actually—but hiking without a backpack and knowing that there would be a hotel and delicious French food and wine at the end of the day made it a deeply romantic, intimate, and powerful time for the two of us. This was something we accomplished together. Hurrah. I was hooked.

Following the week in Corsica, we flew to Monaco and were privileged to witness our two friends marry. The wedding was a once-in-a-lifetime experience, as we watched vows being exchanged on the deck of a yacht as the sun set over the Monaco harbour. We stood in our summer suits fully proud of our friends' commitment to each other. But in all honesty, the highlight of this trip to Europe was putting our brand-new hiking boots to the ground and climbing through unknown hills and forests with a baguette in my day pack.

In honour of the tenth anniversary of our marriage, in 2014, we participated in a guided weeklong hike to Machu Picchu in Peru; the distinction and novelty of this hike is the altitude, which makes breathing very difficult. There is nothing more hilarious than watching a group of fit people walk up a mountainside one tiny step at a time. Coming upon the ancient, lost city of Machu Picchu at sunrise is seared in my memory. We organized it perfectly so that we finished the hike in time to enjoy Inti Raymi—the Festival of the Sun—when the town of Cusco comes alive every June. We were humble guests at this ancient tradition.

Feeling much more experienced and confident, three years ago I offered to do the planning for us without the assistance of a travel company. Bruce was pleased, and I started to wonder if his secret master plan all along had been to make a hiker out of me. It was working. I organized for the two of us to hike the Tour du Mont Blanc, a distance totalling 170 kilometres. This ten-day hike took us through France, to mountaintops in Italy, across Switzerland for a few sunny days, and then back into France in a brilliant circular route. I had it all planned out: where we would stay every night, how many kilometres we would need to walk daily, what landmarks we would pass when. It went brilliantly and smoothly. We walked out of the village of Les Houches, France, one summer morning and carried on up and around the mountain sides of Mont Blanc; ten days later, after walking through three countries, we arrived back at the same village—having experienced the entire distance without the aid of transportation. And we carried everything on our backs. Every step was exhilarating.

We hiked to the base of the Matterhorn in Switzerland in the summer of 2019. There were some days that challenged our resilience: painful elevations were followed by excruciating descents. But the huge shift for me was my confidence. I now found these difficult routes to be thrilling, versus terrifying and unachievable. I discovered that I was passionate about arranging the planning of the hikes—considering all the options and deliberating over every stop, every town, and all the equipment we would need. It went off flawlessly, except for one moment when my exhausted body missed a rock, causing me to stumble forward a few feet and almost be tossed over a cliff, tumbling to my certain death.

For the summer of 2020, we were booked for a full hut-to-hut hike in the Dolomites in Italy. I had dreamed about it, studied it, and booked all the huts. Six months in advance, of course. Thanks to the pandemic, this hike was never realized. I had to cancel all parts of the trip, piece by piece. It was a slow dissolve: COVID chewed away at my favourite activity and left us grounded.

This past summer of 2021, a few months ago, before this emergency Camino was envisioned, we had already decided to "hike local." Abby was in overnight summer camp for five weeks, so Bruce and I flew to Vancouver and conquered the legendary West Coast Trail in British Columbia, Canada. Considered one of the great bucket-list hikes in the world, we took on the challenge. By all reports it would not be an easy hike. Nervously we proceeded. Over seven days, we hiked a challenging obstacle course: rock climbing over jagged shapes, wild ocean clamouring, while the tide was out; enduring the ascent and descent of seventy lengthy ladders; and learning to maneuver metal bucket containers with ourselves inside, over raging rivers. We slept directly on the pebbly ocean beach (careful to check the tide tables the night before so that we wouldn't wake up soaked), using tents that we carried in our large knapsacks. We ate simple meals while sitting on driftwood or rocks; pasta was a constant offering, as we had to carry absolutely everything. And there was very little wine to be had. It was extraordinarily difficult but truly an opportunity of a lifetime.

MORE THAN TWENTY YEARS AGO, I stood on a dock with a life jacket on, fearful. Now I'm hiking solo in a country far from home, my longest trek so far.

I've come a long way—literally and figuratively.

IT'S JUST INFORMATION

As I approach the seaside town of Getaria shortly after getting ahead of the marathon about to begin miles behind me, I notice the imposing San Salvador Eliza cathedral. It's Sunday—prime time for any church—and I hope a visit might help energize the possibility of a connection with my Catholic faith, to understand my conflicting feelings related to the Catholic Church. Maybe time for prayer? Or at least I could obtain a stamp for my passport. I open the gigantic doors and step inside.

It strikes me that the rows of seating, the pews, are sloping downward toward the back. Most churches are on flat ground and, if anything, slope the other way for better sight lines to the altar. The more I look around, the more I notice that this cathedral is no ordinary cathedral—it's bent and twisted. The walls around the altar are disproportionate and not in balance. One side is actually leaning inward when it should bend outward to match the other side. I went to a Catholic school until I was eighteen, so I've been inside many churches in my life. I've never seen a traditional church so askew.

The word "bent" has often been used to describe a gay

person—as in, "The person isn't quite right, he's bent." It's not a kind phrase. I can't focus on anything else here, thinking about this, and instead of going into deep reflection, I busy myself with a quiet laugh. A woman praying on her knees looks up at me at the sound of my laughter. This causes me to exit this most unusual church rather quickly, without obtaining a stamp, and return to the square. There, up above, I see an apartment with a towel hanging out to dry. The towel is made of multiple bright colours in the pattern of a rainbow. Gay people adopted the rainbow as a positive way to be reflected in the world—rainbows are celebratory and hopeful. It's one of our subtle codes. A rainbow flag or sticker on a shop window lets us know it's safe and that gay people are welcome. Much to my surprise, I have just been to the gayest church in Spain—bent and rainbow supported—existing quietly under the radar.

Later, still laughing and hoping I won't be struck down for calling out a Catholic church's gayness, an older man with a cheerful disposition appears, busily tending to his field. He stops his work and comes up to me.

"¿Estás haciendo el Camino? ¿De dónde eres?" he asks. (Are you walking the Camino? Where are you from?)

"Yo soy de Canada!" I announce, proudly.

He can tell by my response that I'm new to the language, but I'm able to keep up, and he keeps the questions coming. He notices I have packed a lunch, since I'm carrying a local shopping bag in one hand. I explain that, since it is *domingo* (Sunday) and stores are *cerrado* (closed), I'm prepared. I use my words for dates, weather, numbers, emotions that I learned in my beginner's Spanish class. We banter back and forth. When he explains that, in a day from now, I need to stock up on food—as there is no market on the way—I completely understand him and appreciate the tip. We speak for about five minutes, with minimal gesturing. I am relaxed, appreciative, and energized. Near the end of our time together, I'm struggling to find the words to express what I want to say, and then they come to me: *"Mucho gusto!"* (Nice to meet you!) He tries to correct me—as in, "Did you mean *'muchas gracias'* (thank you)?" I point to him without hesitation and say, *"No, señor, mucho gusto!"* He bursts into a big smile, understanding now. How far I have come from uttering that simplistic word *"tren"* a mere few days ago.

I think of my Spanish teacher back in Canada.

For the past six months, I have been in night school online through a college program. It was a pandemic hobby to get me focused on something, with the hope that one day I would spend more time in Spanish-speaking countries. When I first signed up for the course, the Camino was nowhere in my immediate plans. Going back to school presented its own challenges—it's been a couple of decades since I was in any sort of formal class setting. But once a week I gathered online with the loveliest gaggle of students—all trying to understand words and phrases virtually and cram them into our existing vocabulary. I adored Maureen, a retiree and a grandmother, who was always game to try anything in class, no matter how confused she might find herself. Tamar and Abed, two gay men originally from the Middle East, had already conquered two languages and now, impressively, were on to their third, and I think of young Lauren, who wanted to learn Spanish simply so that she could speak more easily with her grandmother in Barcelona. We were forced to do it all online, so one evening, near the end, I invited the class to my backyard. We laughed and drank, and we celebrated the beautiful language that we were attempting to learn. Our charismatic teacher, Guillermo, originally from Mexico City, kept us entertained and inspired. I have a long way to go to become fluent, however; standing in this field, I held a real conversation with a Spanish stranger, and I felt totally comfortable for the first time. I think Guillermo would give me an A for this exchange.

◆ ◆ ◆

AN HOUR LATER I descend into the town of Zumaia.

The misty day so far has made for a wet path, but I've managed my way through. Zumaia is another town with a sensational first impression—from up high to the roaring ocean below, a precarious path steeply leads downward. It'll make a perfect lunch stop. This town is a real discovery for me, and it's barely mentioned in the guidebooks. I'm taking in the view of the harbour, imagining where I will stop for my lunch break, while forgetting to concentrate on my feet hitting the cobblestones properly as I descend into town. In the last few metres before the main avenue, feeling like I have safely made the descent, I ungracefully and swiftly fall to the ground. I make an unavoidable loud scream (me at my wimpiest, to say the least) as I tumble toward the rough pavement, my hands attempting to cushion my fall, my knees slamming to the ground regardless. My scream causes people to take notice. Across the street, I see a man look at me with an expression suggesting *oh, please, someone else come along so I don't have to deal with this man, because I don't really care.* Then I hear two men shouting in Spanish as they run toward me. I notice that one man has a small yellow bucket with a red shovel. My first thought as I'm still lying on the ground bleeding is, *How is a red shovel going to help me?* I'm a bit worried that this is serious. However, I look down and deduce that, although the skin is pulled back, the amount of blood is minimal. The kind men take my arms and help me to my feet. Together we examine my leg. It looks worse than it is. I thank them but assure them it's a light wound and I will be alright. They look greatly relieved, as if I have just told them I'm not going to die. I glance over to the man across the street: he's grateful, motions with a slightly supportive wave, and disappears instantly. As I put on my backpack, I look over and see the "bucket man" returning to his children, en route to the beach. I hadn't seen the other family members waiting and watching their dad save the day. May I be more like that person.

Dignity barely intact, I hobble to the town.

Lunch is a delicious ham sandwich with a chocolate croissant, enjoyed while observing a group of canoe club members carrying their crafts overhead, sliding them into the water, and sailing off. My leg appreciates the rest. Though I'm slightly limping now, it doesn't seem like the wound will hold me back.

That said, it turns into a very long day again, and for the last two hours, I have two options: walk along the ocean with killer views, which, according to the guidebook, is "difficult" but "brilliant," or walk inland, which will be "rolling hills and slightly quicker." Coming up with all sorts of great reasons why the inland route will be better for me today, I choose the slightly quicker route. Going in the other direction is a small gaggle of pilgrims who are about to risk the difficult and brilliant way. *Good luck to you,* I think. I'll be in the bar in the town of Deba ahead of all of them. I head onto my slightly quicker path.

About twenty minutes into the dullest section of a hike I've ever encountered, I get angry at myself—I'm walking alone with no other hikers in sight through dull forests alongside a four-lane busy highway. I consider turning back. But it's too late; I've made a choice. Luckily, I recall a golden rule that I used to live by, forgotten these past few years. It's what a great friend and theatre colleague from Calgary, Lesley, always used to say. If things went poorly at the theatre (terrible reviews, for example), she would say, "It's just information." And if things went well at the theatre (huge ticket sales, for example), she'd say it again: "It's just information." It's a way to level things out. I first thought this perspective was greatly frustrating, but it's become a guiding principle for me. I use it in all aspects of my life now, and it helps me avoid self-judgment. Remembering this, I decide to enjoy the route I have chosen.

Day three was an excellent day of discoveries and rediscoveries.

I will step more carefully on wet stones.

And next time I will take the ocean route when offered.

It's just information.

PANIC

As I leave the town of Deba on the fourth day, the morning presents sunshine for the first time since I landed in Spain. I've been grateful for the light mist and clouds, which kept the temperature down while I walked up high on mountain ranges fully exposed to the sky. But I won't deny that this morning, discovering the sunrise breaking through the clouds and revealing the splendour of the ocean, I welcome the overdue sun. I have become used to the cloudy days—deciding poetically (but not cleverly) that this is a metaphor for my mind.

In the centre of Deba, there's an ancient bridge dating back to 1863. The core of it is disintegrating into the sea. It's not an enormous bridge, but vital to the flow and access into the town. As I walk nearer, I discover a full-scale renovation in process. What they've set up seems unconventional: they've erected a temporary scaffold bridge directly on top of the rotting one, so that everyone can carry on while the restoration is undertaken. It's a sight to behold—this two-level bridge, the past and the future. It seems to me a clever solution to a complicated problem. Fix the past while carrying on with the present—another Camino metaphor in disguise?

• • •

My brain is still rather empty of serious, self-reflective thoughts. I would have imagined that, once I started walking on the Camino, the questions of life back home would overwhelm me. Is it avoidance? I'm not sure. The offer of a journey like this is that it is filled with the wonderment of novelty—there is something new to experience and digest with every step. Not one moment has been a repetition of anything I have ever seen before. The more I walk softly (thanks, Helene), the more I can focus on the details around me. It's truly a case of soaking up the journey, not the destination. I'm grateful for this, as the destination is still a daunting four weeks and over six hundred kilometres away.

The route today promises to be hilly but straightforward. And it will be only twenty-five kilometres, requiring six to eight hours to keep myself entertained. Two hours into the hike, high on a hill, I pass by a closed *albergue* that would have been a welcome rest for pilgrims. It is secluded and very basic, but full of charm. Wood tables and chairs are stacked outside under a canopy of ancient tree branches. Clear light bulbs are strung above the garden, for evening dining. And yet, the whole area is deserted. I'm guessing that they weren't able to open this season. Out here in the open air, it makes me wonder why they didn't even try. Wouldn't it have been worth it, even at a reduced capacity? Isn't something better than nothing? COVID is wreaking havoc everywhere. I think of the work lost, and the people affected by it. And it reminds me of my theatre back home and of the idea of performing half of a play to a handful of audience members. No one wants that.

So I surrender to the reality: these people did what they had to do. By all reports, many of these places set up for pilgrims may never reopen. They weren't intended to be profit centres, and with all the restrictions, it's proving to be too difficult to proceed. This makes me feel a little more connected to the world—in a not-so-positive sort of way. Until now on this walk, I had been mostly able to think COVID away. I've avoided all newspapers and the world online. However, today it becomes clear that the destructive effect of the pandemic is here too, on the Camino.

A bit later, I notice that the hike is becoming progressively harder; the mud is getting soggier, the rocks larger, and the elevation steeper. It is all becoming incredibly tiring and difficult to navigate. About an hour into this new stretch, I decide that this is by far the hardest section I've hiked on this Camino.

It feels uncharacteristically difficult, in fact. That should have been a clue.

When will it ever end? I noticed the other day that, even though I don't have cell coverage for my phone, I can still track my location. Even better, my exact position is visible on my Camino app. Every now and then, I check my phone to see if the bouncing ball (me) is showing on the yellow squiggly line (the route). It is always a relief to see that I am on track.

The next town is supposed to be two kilometres away. If the day is going to keep on like this, it will be a long, arduous day. *I should be there by now,* I keep thinking over and over. This is not making sense. To reassure myself, I turn on the Camino app. For the first thirty seconds, my little bouncing marker doesn't appear. I don't exist. Then when it does appear, I discover that, according to this technology, I'm in the middle of a forest to the west of where the Camino route is—clearly far from the yellow line. I took a wrong turn somewhere (back at that abandoned *albergue*?) and now am considerably off track. Trying not to worry, I walk on, hoping my error will simply correct itself and I will be headed directly back onto the path. Strangely, the bouncing ball is moving farther west, and the more I move, the more in the wrong direction it goes. I'm completely lost and come to realize that I have been making it worse for many kilometres.

I panic.

My heart starts to race, the smile on my face drops away. I'm no longer worried about the difficulty of the trail. My focus switches to survival. I'm on some other path (possibly on a serious hiking route—the challenging GR-10, a sixty-day hike that crosses France and Spain—but currently going where?). I'm hours away from getting back on track. The markers I have been following are yellow and red. And not arrows. I stupidly thought, *Well, that's close enough.* I suspect the GR-10 is marked in these colours, so I am not on the Camino at present. An arrow is an arrow. Oops.

The path does not relent, and as I'm still in the forest and unable to see much around me, I decide to go deeper and deeper. I hope that the bouncing ball is leading me somewhere in parallel to the Camino, and so for that reason, I might be safe. It's amazing how I talk myself into this logic, especially when I'm lost. I always understood it was difficult to get too lost on the Camino. Arguably, I don't think going back will be worth it—it would add a gruelling five hours to the day, which would certainly mean a midnight arrival in the next town, making this potentially a fourteen-hour hiking day. As I continue on, the path becomes more overgrown. The sky is more difficult to see, leaves and branches overwhelming everything. I haven't seen anyone for hours, and I won't likely be seeing anyone out here today.

When the trees open into a clearing, a view emerges—and what I see causes me to scream, "OH FUUUUUUUUUUUCK!"

I have managed to hike myself up an extremely high mountain.

No wonder it was so difficult to climb. This is not good. In all of my preparation for the Camino, I never imagined going off the path. It hadn't dawned on me that I could find myself alone at the top of a mountain with no clear way out. Suddenly I feel incredibly vulnerable, exposed, and stupid. Feelings of failure overwhelm me. I sit down, drink a small amount of water, and try to breathe.

After the panic and the swearing subside, I carry on forward. I notice the brush around me looking withered and dead in places, and the presence of clear-cutting in some of the area is obvious. Clear-cutting on a mountain top? Where am I? Distracted by this, it dawns on me that even the yellow and red land markers have stopped.

I'm now lost while being lost. Is that even possible?

My heart racing, I see that the path goes up higher, so I try to convince myself, *Well, maybe it's just up there.* That's when American travel writer Bill Bryson and his book *A Walk in the Woods*, about his adventures on the Appalachian Trail, pop into my head. He writes about going off-trail and losing sight of the way markings. It is the worst thing one could do. It's simple: never go off-trail. Getting more lost is not the right direction.

Even though I believe that turning around and going back to the last sign is a waste of time, I retreat in search of a marker. Three hundred feet back, the first sign I see is not an arrow but a large "X" indicating not to take the route I just took.

Message received—belatedly.

"Ughhhhh." Frustration. I had walked right past the warning sign.

I scan the forest in hopes of a marking that will show me the correct direction. And close enough to touch, two feet away, I discover a little sign pointing easterly. The good news is I'm not doubly lost now—just back to simply being lost. I'm back on track on the mysterious path (it's the GR-10, I am now convinced), but at least the evil bandits hiding in the forest awaiting their next victim aren't going to capture a directionless theatre director anytime soon. Well, not yet.

My heart starts to race.

After twenty more minutes wandering forward, a junction

appears. I can see the official route in the distance: it's across a valley and up a ridge on an adjoining hillside. If I trust what my eyes are seeing—a bunch of dirt roads up a mountain just in view—I might be able to reconnect. Now totally off any plan or official-looking route (except a pretty wide dirt road), I decide to go for it. Sorry, Bill Bryson. The path is in the open, so it at least feels comforting to know what my potential plan (or should I say mistake?) will be. After ninety gruelling minutes of an uphill climb across the ridge, I find my way back to the official route. When I see my first yellow arrow, I scream with glee and the panic subsides.

The big yellow arrows seem to be laughing at me and lighting the way like a Vegas runway, saying, *This way, moron, this way.* I'm incredibly relieved, and grateful that I have survived this stupid mistake. Multiple pilgrims pass me with a look of confusion: *Who are you? Why haven't we seen you yet today?* I carry on—not moving my feet too far ahead until the next distinct Camino arrow is in plain sight. I walk on with a laser focus. Very straightforward country roads, no scrambling, no confusion or doubt. I will watch signs more closely and keep the bouncing circle near to me.

It's just information, I try to repeat to myself over and over.

Eventually I arrive at the town of Markina and the hostel I have booked. The building is a smartly crafted barnlike structure. Stepping inside, I discover a large group of hikers of all ages. We exchange our polite greetings. It is serene. And tonight I sleep in a bunk-bed room with twenty-five genuine pilgrims. All the windows are wide open, and masks are worn walking to and from our beds.

It's a surreal setting, but I feel much safer to not be alone tonight, and grateful to be among other humans.

WELCOME—MOVE
FORWARD—PUSH

SOMEONE ELSE'S ALARM CLOCK wakes me up this morning. Six in the morning and all these pilgrims tucked in their bunks slowly come to life. I've heard about this ritual: hostel mates gingerly moving through the dark, some with headlamps alight, quietly packing their things to go. I decide to wait a bit and watch this dance—it's quite a light show—red and blue and white mini-lights bouncing off the ceiling.

Eventually I join the action and pack up quietly. I look down at a lone empty plastic bag and wish it well—I don't want to be a noise maker, so I leave it to its fate on the floor. As I look at all these people generously moving in silence, I have two thoughts: *maybe these are my people; no surfboards in sight.* But the bigger, sadder reflection I have is how we were all together but never did gel as a group.

Usually at these places there are nightly communal meals. The food is passed, wine is poured, and stories are told. Often the host asks everyone to share with those assembled why they are walking the Camino. It's a deeply powerful gathering and bonds are formed, I'm told. This year, thanks to the pandemic, the hosts are not allowed to serve food or to seat us so closely indoors. Even the breakfast (usually a coffee and bun) is cancelled. So the key opportunities, likely the most magical moments of the stay, are lost.

Last night part of me wanted to speak up and ask everyone what their story was—but it's not my place, and it is not my show. I stayed quiet. I had a few stifled, short conversations, but all in all, it was a hushed, unconnected evening. I felt like I hid last night and should have tried harder. What was I so afraid of? I can command a large group of people if I'm directing a theatre production, but I'm nervous and shy around a few people standing at the bathroom sinks.

Regret and failure fill my being. It puts me in a rough mood to start my day.

While yesterday's adventure in the woods had a happy ending and I certainly will be better for it going forward, I still feel vulnerable today. I don't want to be lost again. I can and should do better—how difficult can following signs be? I pout quietly as I begin today's walk in the half light. I don't want to stop for coffee yet. I pass many open bars, but I can't muster the courage to confront another person. It just reminds me of the loneliness of the hostel. I'll walk off this feeling, I hope, leaving behind the sadness that is building.

After moving through a second town full of bars where coffee is available, I decide to keep on walking to the third town, assuring myself there will be options at my disposal there. The physical aspect of walking seems more difficult today, and the misty rain is causing the path and the rocks to be quite slippery. It reminds me of falling and bleeding a couple of days ago. I'm tired and it's not even ten in the morning yet. My dark thoughts escalate: *maybe this hike was a mistake and it's not actually for me.* I haven't even survived one week yet, so how in the hell am I going to make it through another four? Step by step I become haunted with familiar thoughts of sadness and failure. And so, when I come upon the third town, Munitibar, and discover that the only bar in town is closed, I feel defeated in a way I have not previously experienced on this trip. Not because of the coffee, but because of my failure to navigate this life.

I'VE ALWAYS BEEN ABLE TO SOLDIER ON when the going got tough. I've always had a storehouse of energy to push through difficult times. My enthusiasm and positivity typically have been a bridge across conflict and turmoil. I'm a happy person, dammit. But during this time, my resilience has been worn away. My ability to rebound has been lost.

A wise friend of mine, Guy, told me recently that it was clear to him what the problem is: my pilot light is out. The flame that inspires and keeps me energized—live theatre— has been cancelled. My imagination hasn't been engaged for months. My creativity hasn't been called for. During this crisis, we've been focused on paying bills at the theatre, not making art. Theatre globally has been put on pause. Like so many industries that have been hampered, theatre had to shut down completely almost everywhere. Picture an actor on Broadway, a lighting designer in Beijing, a stage carpenter in Latvia— most of them are still not working anywhere.

And even if the theatre world can survive this pandemic and a comeback is possible, I've woken up to the reality that the world doesn't need or want another older white male theatre director, nor should it. Everything that I had organized my career and identity around was suddenly seemingly obsolete. My profession and my main creative expression in life are threatened with extinction, and I wonder if my place in the theatre is no longer relevant. I can feel the rightness of this—it's a thrilling development for the arts—but I also feel a paralyzing grief. While hoping for the theatre's survival, I also realize that it needs to evolve into something more equitable, with leadership from people who have been denied access for far too long. Which feels possibly like evolution without the likes of me.

Today a familiar feeling returns: helplessness. I can't do a simple thing such as buy a cup of coffee. The world that I ran away from has finally appeared, and the glorious distraction of this past week has dropped away. Feelings of being worthless resurface. I think about going to the nearest airport and flying home.

Farther up the hill, I arrive at the Monasterio de Zenarruza. The courtyard is deserted. There is an imposing door on this church that seems very difficult to open—no handle to be seen. I can't figure my way in. On this large slab of wood is a sign with one statement, translated into nine languages. It reads:

> Ongi etorri, irekita dago, bultzatu.
> Bienvenido, pase adelante, empuje.
> Welcome, move forward, push.
> Benvenuti, fatti avanti, spingi.
> Willkommen, vorwärts gehen, drücken.
> Bienvenue, avance, pousse.
> Hoş geldin, ileri git, it.
> Bine aţi venit, mergeţi înainte, împingeţi.
> -欢迎，前进，推动.

I see my instructions: "Welcome, move forward, push."

I'm struck by a thought: *Is this a directive about a door or a useful motto for the remainder of my hike? Or the remainder of my life?* Feeling strangely hesitant, I move forward and then I push on the door. This gigantic monolith of a structure beautifully glides open revealing a perfectly realized interior, a stunningly preserved, empty cathedral. I walk in, sit down in a church pew, and start to cry.

And cry.

"Move forward, push."

I just don't know that I can.

Three months ago I found myself randomly sobbing out loud, then going down to my knees on the kitchen floor, collapsing in a ball of sorrow. Why was it always the kitchen floor? I couldn't process the details of my sadness. It seemed to me that speaking about it might break me open, and not allow me to ever be put back together. And besides, this wasn't me: I wasn't a dark soul. I was the positive, spirited jokester.

I kept all these thoughts to myself.

Shortly after one of those crying sessions on the floor, I was sitting in Deb's office, along with Suzanne, the director of development of the Grand Theatre and a great human. These two have always been my champions and are masters at turning my ideas into reality, while laughing at my inane jokes. They had also watched me descend into dark thoughts and feelings of worthlessness over many previous months. The pressure of the job was eating me alive, so when I blurted out, "If I can't figure this out, I think I'll jump off a bridge," there was an abrupt silence in the room. I was taken aback that I had said it—mostly that I had said it out loud. That was something no coworker wants to hear. I crossed a line and put them in an awkward position. And it was true: Over the previous few weeks, walking over large bridges, I would look around and imagine the best place to jump from. I'd always factor in that I wouldn't want to land on the traffic below. I didn't need to kill others in the pursuit of my own demise.

That afternoon, I went home and wrote my resignation. I wouldn't have theatre anymore, but maybe I could still hold on to my life.

I met with Anita, the board chair, and handed her the piece of paper with my resignation. She took a moment to digest what I had just told her, but she was clear in her opinion.

Using grace and calm, she disagreed with my stance, my idea, and the piece of paperwork in front of her. I had explained to her that it simply was time for me to move on. She told me, "I don't believe you are done with the Grand Theatre. I know you have more to give and that the mission you have set out for yourself is not complete here. I've seen the passion in your eyes."

I was shocked. She didn't talk about the Grand's needs and how I would disrupt things. She talked about me. My dreams, unfulfilled.

"Anita, you don't understand. This is more than I can bear, and it's best for my health. These COVID times have been unrelenting and painful for everyone, I understand that. But I can only speak about myself. I'm simply not coping," I blurted out, my voice cracking. What I didn't say was that I spent my days sobbing on the kitchen floor.

With that, she relented, and promised to support whatever I wanted. Talking to Anita sent me into further sadness, for now I was disappointing her as well. What a mess upon a mess I had created. The day after we talked, I went on an incredibly long walk through the streets alone and had to be careful not to step into traffic—my brain was in such a fuzzy state. It scared the hell out of me: I wasn't in pain; I was numb. I wasn't feeling anything.

Miraculously, the next day I woke up with an idea that I had never ever considered: it might be possible for me to stay on longer at the theatre if, and only if, I took a break immediately. If I couldn't run away from the theatre forever, maybe I could run away from the world for a while and attempt a restore and reset.

My problem-solving husband Bruce suggested that, instead of the two of us dreaming about hiking the Camino in Spain a few years from now, as we had been, I needed to go right away.

And solo.

"You can cover Abby for five weeks alone, while I go off on a hike?" I asked in total disbelief. "That's a long time to be away."

"Yes, of course," Bruce said. "But only if you go into this with your full self. You can't feel the guilt of leaving us. You need to lean in and give this your everything. I know you. Make this matter. This is better than watching you collapse. And promise me you'll drink copious amounts of Rioja wine and eat lots of *tapas*." Bruce's offer was bold.

Stunned by this option that I'd never considered, I asked Deb and Suzanne their thoughts before going back to the board chair. They were unanimous: they would support whatever I wanted. "Can I drive you to the airport?" Suzanne offered seconds after I proposed the idea.

I called Anita with a compromise: I would stay on if the board of directors allowed me a five-week sabbatical immediately.

"First of all, yes, I think a sabbatical is a perfect idea," Anita began. I could hear the relief in her voice. "What would you like to do with the time, do you think?"

"It's called the Camino de Santiago."

"Where's that?"

"Spain."

I heard a little laugh through the phone. "You don't do anything simply, do you, Dennis?"

"I'll need to confirm this with the board, of course," Anita said. "But I can tell you right now we will support this. I'm so pleased. I just need you to do one thing."

Hesitation overwhelmed me momentarily. There's a catch.

"I need you to allow me to rip up your resignation."

With a half smile and a relieved sigh, I agreed.

As I LOOK AROUND THIS EMPTY CHURCH, pristine and

beautifully well kept, I realize that it's been a month since I've sobbed on the kitchen floor, so crying again in this vacant church scares me. I was hopeful this sabbatical would stop the flow of tears. However, after the initial sobs, I take a deep breath and realize this crying feels different: less like anguish for something I cannot change and more like an acceptance of my situation. It's certainly a release—of what, I'm not sure. But possibly more importantly, it feels like an opening.

I notice in the corner a series of candles sitting in red votive jars, the type you light when you are thinking of someone. I go over and light one of the remaining few candles. No donation box, no payment required. My mom comes to mind.

"Yogi, I need you today."

No one in English-speaking Canada could pronounce her name, Huguette, so when she joined the Armed Forces, she was given a nickname. For some reason I will never know, she was named after the famous American baseball player Yogi Berra. And I was the only kid allowed to call her by this name instead of only Mom. She and I had many special arrangements.

I haven't prayed in years, and certainly not in a church. But today I attempt a little prayer.

"Yogi, I'm here in Spain. You've likely watched me struggle these several months, and now I've thrown myself into this trek. Am I in over my head? If you were here, you'd set me straight—you'd tell me to stop crying and get going. The Lord doesn't want you to wait, you'd say. And you'd probably tell me you are proud of me and give me a warm hug. I'm feeling that right now. But my loneliness is kicking in, as is my fear of failure. I still want to do this pilgrimage. I really do. Can you be with me—just to see me through this? I'll borrow your fortitude. Please help me today, Mom."

The silence is broken as the large entry door moves again and a man from the church office walks directly over to me and asks me if I want my stamp for my Camino credentials.

Until now, I have been successful obtaining stamps from hotels and restaurants. It's been difficult to find churches open during the pandemic with staff available to stamp credentials. I follow him to the church office and receive my stamp. This offering catches me off guard—that the man reached out to me versus me coming to him. A pattern is broken, and I'm welcomed in. Maybe he saw my tear-stained cheeks or my red eyes? Did he hear my crying?

Back in the churchyard, I notice three people I met at the hostel last night, standing and staring at the imposing door, looking nervous, just as I had. In uncharacteristic fashion, I speak up loudly from behind them. "You just need to walk forward. And push," I call out. They look back at the door. One of the women hesitantly approaches the imposing building. She lifts her right hand and pushes the door. It opens as if a miracle has occurred. They thank me, relieved.

Welcome.

Move forward.

Push.

FRESH RIPE PEARS

I DECIDE NOT TO HEAD TO THE NEAREST AIRPORT TODAY but, instead, to move forward.

Coming out of a forest an hour after leaving the Monasterio de Zenarruza, I see a striking house with a garden overflowing with wild tulips and periwinkle, clearly curated and tended with love. An older woman with a deeply summer-tanned face alive with wrinkles appears on her porch and is looking directly at me. She must be about eighty years old and is wearing a light summer linen dress with the slightest flower pattern, possessing the warmth of many decades of a well-lived life. I smile and walk on. In the quiet of the morning, the woman calls me back. I pause for a moment and think of my mom, who would want me to engage, not be afraid, and talk to this woman no matter how nervous I might be. I turn around, and I walk back to her with a big smile on my face and say hello.

The conversation begins easily enough.

"*¿Eres un peregrino?*" she asks.

"*Si. Yo soy de Canada,*" I say.

She wants to show me her gorgeous orchard of pear trees: there must be fifty of them. This woman invites me to pick some for my journey today. Even though I explain to her that I speak *un poquito* Spanish, she carries on with the questions. After I pick my first few pears, she screams, *"Más!"* I laugh out loud and agree: *"Más!"* ("more" sounds like another motto to adopt on this journey). After we pick the low-hanging fruit, I goofily point to a branch high up and rich with offerings. I gesture as if to say, *Too bad we can't get those.* And without missing a beat, she grabs my walking pole from my hand, goes over to the tree, and starts smacking at the fruit—and pears rain down all around us. *"Más! Más! Más!"* We both laugh in unison.

I take a bite of this ripe, fresh fruit, picked from this lovingly created orchard. Its soft texture and sweet taste are a welcome refreshment. The woman wants to know how much I will be walking. I tell her that it will be over *"ochocientos kilometros"* (eight hundred kilometres). She laughs again—this time as if to suggest it's impossible—waves her hand at me and walks away, shaking her head joyfully as she disappears.

If Yogi were alive and she had pears to offer, I like to think she'd share them with people as they walked by.

Less than thirty minutes later, two other people from the hostel appear and initiate a conversation. "Are you ok?" the kind woman asks. A bold question to throw at a stranger. They're a super-fit German couple who are both running and walking the Camino (impressively alternating one day running, then two days walking). "I missed having coffee this morning," I feebly respond. They point out a café hidden around the block they just discovered, and the coffee I had given up on for the day materializes. I race over and drink a *café con leche* quickly and happily.

I'm now bouncing down the path, marvelling at how my day is unfolding and morphing, when yet another man from the hostel appears. He initiates a conversation, and we begin to walk together. He is from France and is awfully handsome:

slender, dark hair, and deep-blue eyes. He is quiet and intense and has a gorgeous smile. So deliciously French. When
he asks my name, I think I blush. His name is Roma. He lives
in Normandy and works with farmers to develop progres-
sive farming techniques. As we walk together, we talk world
politics, the Camino, and COVID, all using stilted English to
guide us through. He jokes, "Your leader in Canada is a good-
looking man who came in strong but now has been found to
be less competent and less likable. Wait a minute, that's our
president!" We laugh at his clever observation. France's president Emmanuel Macron and Canada's prime minister Justin
Trudeau do share similarities. . . .

Roma is impressed with a small farm we pass by and points
out something he describes as synchronistic farming. The
corn in the field is being grown alongside—and with—beans
at their base. The two grow very well together. I'd never heard
of this and certainly would not have understood this myself
without him pointing it out. As the terrain becomes more tax-
ing, I can't keep up, so Roma tells me he will look for me ahead.
I imagine that is the last I will see of him and walk alone happily, trying to digest the unexpected offerings of the day so far.
At the top of a hill, I see Roma hiking and notice that he looks
back toward me as he stops at a bar. I can't tell if he wants me
to have lunch with him or move on. It feels like a mixed message. I decide to walk on—our little romance complete. (I have
a habit of falling for people—male or female—many times
throughout a day.)

An hour later I see a gathering of people: two women and
a pile of kids. The older woman waves: she has a question. The
woman brings over her younger companion, who speaks perfect English. She will translate for her group. They want to
know about an alternative hike to a waterfall that would be
better for the children. Wanting to encourage their field trip,
I happily suggest the best path to take, based on what I can

surmise about the area. I am an expert in Spanish trails now, or so it seems. Probing the woman who speaks excellent English, I learn that she is from Alberta and now lives in Bilbao just down the road. A fellow Canadian! I'm super playful with the young kids, and a five-year-old boy says "thank you" to me in a lovely Spanish accent as I walk on.

Walking up a cliff overlooking the valley below, I meet a second British woman on the Camino. Emma is thirty years old and knows Canada well, having worked in much-loved tourist destinations such as Tofino in British Columbia and Banff in Alberta. She's on her own, improvising her Camino details as she goes—nothing planned. She loves the adventures of the unknown. We have a delightful conversation, and eventually she walks on.

A few hours later I arrive in the city of Guernica feeling energized and renewed. This city was heavily bombed by Nazi Germany, and renowned artist Pablo Picasso represented this in his acclaimed 1937 antiwar painting aptly called *Guernica*. The painting now hangs in a museum in Madrid. It's powerful to walk the streets seeing the evidence of the destruction and subsequent reconstruction—and knowing that Picasso was inspired to create because of it.

I notice Emma again. She's sitting on a patio enjoying a much-deserved beer. She waves me over and invites me to sit with her. Emma insists on buying me a drink. We have a big, spirited, open, playful chat about our lives.

Today I needed companionship, a sense of purpose, a confidence to move forward, and a cold glass of beer at the end of the day with a new friend. The Camino (and my mom) provided.

ONE THING PLANNED

I WAKE UP EARLY TODAY WITH NERVOUS ANTICIPATION, knowing that this is going to be my longest hiking day so far. I will be walking thirty-one kilometres to the city of Bilbao. And I don't want to be late. I have a ticket for a concert on the outdoor terrace of the renowned Guggenheim Museum Bilbao. These concerts happen infrequently in the summer; there is one tonight, and thanks to my advanced planning, I bought one of the last seats. I'm excited. But first I have to walk there.

I jump out of bed and begin packing Gregory, who feels strangely lighter every day—though his contents don't actually change. I fill the knapsack efficiently and quickly now, having figured out an order and a place for every item. I pick up my phone and see that I have an email waiting. I'm not receiving email from work, as I have disabled delivery of those (and am not even tempted to look); however, Bruce and I are staying in occasional contact this way. We both decided not to communicate too regularly. No phone calls or detailed updates—to begin with at least. And with the six-hour time-zone difference, our daily patterns are out of sync anyway.

The email involves our daughter, Abby. Bruce writes to tell me that the overnight camp where she's been for a month has called, and there is a COVID scare and possible outbreak. She may have contracted the disease and needs to be picked up as soon as possible. Her stay there will be cut short.

Summer camp typically is Abby's happiest time of the year. She loves nature and the outdoors—and is a terrific swimmer who could live in the water all day long. She's outgoing, charming, and strong. And not afraid to meet people and to help out as needed. We were relieved when camps agreed to open this summer, given that they were shuttered last year. We counted the months and weeks leading to camp. In fact, for a late-July start date, her packing began in January. It was one of the lifelines for our family—something to look forward to. And now she would be coming home early—with more unstructured time to fill.

The stress of work is not the only reason I have come to Spain. While it is the most public aspect, it doesn't compare with what has been happening in my home life. The subject I have been avoiding in my thoughts is how my kid has struggled through COVID and has taken it out on her two parents constantly for the last year. I know I am not alone: it's likely that most parents have found this to be an especially challenging time.

The last six months of living with my usually outgoing and social eleven-year-old as she struggled to cope with isolation and online learning have been one of the most difficult experiences in my life. We've seen an angry and violent side, and a fully withdrawn side. She went from being a girl to an adolescent. Often I collapsed after she yelled an obscenity at me, ran up the stairs, and slammed her bedroom door (which was coming off its hinges from all the abuse she was giving it). The times I spent on the kitchen floor sobbing a few months ago were connected to those outbursts. Abby was not managing well, and I didn't know what to do for her. I questioned my parenting skills constantly.

Some days I cried for my theatre, some days I cried for my child.

When I spoke of this to friends, they reminded me that she is a preteen girl and suggested that it comes with the territory. It certainly feels more epic and painful than simply "a phase." We've tried every version of counselling, and a variety of pills for her. I have never felt so useless as a parent. And I feel deeply for the pain she is going through. We're sharing similar stresses, and they're coming out in such different ways. I wish I could help her, as I wish I could help myself.

Just before camp, we felt like we had things in order, and now that she was with other kids on a daily basis, we hoped her moods and energy would level out. Early reports from camp this summer were that she liked it enough, but the rules and regulations made it harder for her to connect and play freely. However, she was outdoors and appreciated it. I left for the Camino feeling confident about her summer plans.

Bruce explained in his email that he would be cancelling work for the day and driving north to pick her up. His final sentence was "please don't worry."

Looking after my mental health has been a part-time job for Bruce. He navigated me through this past chunk of time with as much positivity as he could muster. We both knew I had hit rock bottom, though, in the spring when I collapsed on the floor in the kitchen for the tenth time and, while sitting on the tiles, said very quietly, "Tell me what to do." That's all. "Tell me what to do." With that, the much-discussed idea of taking antidepression medication returned. He called the doctor immediately and held the phone to my ear. I asked for pills. On the phone the doctor said, "I know we talked about this recently. And these feelings have grown for you? Just too many things to deal with?"

To which I agreed. Three hours later I started on antidepressants, for the first time in my life. Within a week I felt the new sensation of disconnection. Abby was arguing with us, and I turned to Bruce calmly and stated, "You'll have to solve this one. I'm not feeling anything." While the reprieve from the helplessness was appreciated, this didn't feel right. Once the Camino was decided, I took myself slowly off the pills. I didn't want to experience the Camino through that lens.

So when Bruce asked me not to worry in the email today, before I set off to Bilbao, it was a gentle reminder of how I do tend to. . . .

NOT SURPRISINGLY, I START my walk feeling defeated today, worrying about Abby.

I have no choice but to keep moving. I have an event to attend tonight—which now seems absurd, given the morning news, but an event nonetheless. My thoughts all day long are with my poor daughter, her plans interrupted again, alone with only one parent by her side. And I feel very far away.

These days are proving to be roller coasters. Yesterday I was feeling present and connected. Today I'm feeling guilt and remorse because I should be home in Canada. Attending a concert tonight seems selfish. That feeling is resolved for me soon enough when an email arrives directly from the museum. Due to some COVID-protocol problems, they are "very sorry to report" that tonight's concert is now cancelled.

There goes the plan.

Discouraged, I hike on, crossing through some of the drabbest industrial streets and highways. I never walk through the outskirts of cities like this, but here it's becoming a regular pattern. The final three hours of the day involve climbing up and over a rather brutal and rough hill. Industrial, noisy, dirty, and uneven. Not unlike the thoughts in my head.

I stop by the busy roadside and break our agreement: I dial Bruce's cell phone.

"You didn't have to call," Bruce says.

"I know. I just wanted to check in. And you can walk with me for a bit."

"I love that. I'll walk with you while we talk." Back in Canada, Bruce puts on his shoes and heads out the door of our house. We are now walking together—virtually. I can hear the sounds of our neighbourhood: dogs barking, neighbours greeting Bruce, his footsteps as he walks down the street. He continues, "Well, we're back home. The seven hours in the car to get there and back were uneventful. They did a quick test and she's negative. But they've decided to shut things down nonetheless." I breathe out, relieved that she's healthy.

"How are her spirits?" I ask.

"She's ok, actually. I guess part of all this COVID upheaval is that no place feels entirely the same as it was. Camp was totally different for her. With all the social-distancing rules and masks, she was finding it hard to connect with other campers, which was meant to be the whole appeal of being there."

"Alright. I guess that was a bit predictable," I offer. "What are you going to do with her for all this extra time?"

"I'll figure something out. Don't worry. How's that rock of yours?"

"He's excellent. Quiet little thing, actually."

"They usually are," Bruce says. "Found a place to leave him behind yet?"

"Nope." We chat for an hour. I make a mental note to myself to find the rock that I have forgotten about or am currently avoiding. I'll keep him closer by.

I arrive in Bilbao after a record-breaking eight hours (pretty good coverage of thirty-one kilometres). I'm right on time—with nowhere to be.

BEAUTIFUL CAMINO

DEPRIVED OF AN OUTDOOR CONCERT at the Guggenheim Bilbao last night, I'm still hopeful and determined to make it there and have a lovely day at the museum.

When I see a movie or attend a live performance or, in this case, explore a museum, I prefer to know as little as possible before I experience it. I absolutely hate it when a well-meaning friend says to me, "The movie is brilliant, and the ending is so shocking. . . ." I have been known to put my hands over my ears and sing loudly to drown out these types of conversations. Isn't that the whole point of having experiences in life? To discover things for yourself? On the Camino I have been careful to distinguish between what I need to know for my safety and what should be a discovery. A few pilgrims have tried to be helpful: "When you turn the corner, you're going to be amazed!" Or, "You'll love the architecture of that town." Really? Will I? How do you know what my reaction's going to be? In other words, I step toward the Guggenheim knowing very little. This is the one area I haven't researched and prepped. I come happily unprepared.

The moment the building comes into view, I'm astounded by the scale of it.

I'm standing at the River Nervión, looking at this expansive building in the form of an undulating sculpture. Even from a distance, it dominates the landscape. I cross the river using a pedestrian bridge crafted with extensive wires and an equally undulating walkway. The bridge complements the museum perfectly, and I instantly recognize the work of its Spanish architect, Santiago Calatrava.

When I was living in Alberta in 2012, I witnessed the construction and installation of a stylish red bridge designed by Calatrava, called the Peace Bridge. The price tag was twenty-five million dollars—highly controversial for a pedestrian bridge. I watched it being built, walking by it almost daily. I marvelled at the whimsy and also enjoyed that some people were disturbed by its unique shape. I thought that was a great sign—people were talking about art. It officially opened with great fanfare, and six months later it made the list of top things to see and experience in Calgary. And it still is.

I walk across the bridge that is wonderfully familiar, and as I open the front doors of the museum, I get a powerful sense that this is going to be an extraordinary visit. There is nothing usual or predictable about this place. No straight lines but, instead, soaring ceilings, brilliant winding staircases, and gigantic views through the enormous glass walls. I feel my whole body open into an energized state of imagination—my mind and heart begin to dance with the building. I haven't felt such a rush in a very long time.

Architect and fellow Canadian Frank Gehry has created a dramatic adventure.

The building houses the art, but it also is an interactive piece of art in and of itself. It begs me to take my camera out and shoot wild angles and images. As I explore, my imagination expands, inviting me to float through the building. At times I become silent, but I also find myself moving about speedily and pointing randomly and laughing audibly as I ingest multiple sensations. My smile is plastered to my face—not even my mask can hide my facial excitement. I'm sure I look like a buffoon to anyone watching me.

I find one enormous football-field-sized room to be particularly joyful. *Torqued Ellipses* by Richard Serra is a permanent exhibit of walls created in a mazelike fashion. As a room of museum attendees, we are invited to get lost among the curved walls. Meandering through, looking for odd angles to photograph as I go, I observe gleeful kids and adults getting lost among this art. One man is having more fun taking photographs of his little daughter than the child is running about the maze. At this moment, they are both children.

Everyone plays.

It reminds me of the piece by Christo that was created in Central Park in New York City in 2005 called *The Gates*. Christo was known for wild and wacky art installations, such as wrapping buildings in plastic. Bruce and I were living in New York at the time and were told that large steel frames with bright-orange plastic panels for people to walk through— seven thousand of them—were going to be set up throughout the park. In February! I thought it was a rather stupid idea— that is, until I went for a walk and watched people create art with their cameras. And that was before the ease of camera phones. The bleakness of winter juxtaposed against the colour and life of humans was striking. This was the happiest I had seen New Yorkers in our four years of living there. That's when I understood the importance of involving the viewer directly in the experience, whenever possible.

I glide up the stairs in the Guggenheim and discover a large exhibit called *Moving on from Trauma*. Using the Spanish flu pandemic of 1918 as its reference point, it examines how people emerged from the pandemic with the energy to create the roaring twenties. The exhibit points out that it was called the Spanish flu pandemic only because Spain was the first to officially identify it as a significant situation. The expansive exhibit shows how art houses emerged, artists began to create, and people became animated and reborn out of a great sense of need. What a brilliant bridge to our times. It's hopeful: we'll get through this, it seems to suggest. In one corner, a cabaret hall is set up: round tables and a dance floor dominate. Projected on the floor in many languages is the phrase "Take the stage and dance." Indeed. And yes, people are encouraged to dance here at the Guggenheim—with their masks on, of course.

With this exhibit I also watch an incredibly uplifting silent film showing all the live theatre that was created—through vaudeville, spectacle, and dance—during the roaring twenties. The only way to view the film is to enter a room, lay on the carpet, and look up. The movie is projected on the ceiling. Oh, how many times have I been in a museum and wanted to lie down for a moment. I find my section of carpet, and I turn my eyes upward. It's a delicious experience. And I can feel my heart opening: behind my mask, I'm beaming from ear to ear.

As I return to the main floor, feeling charged and delighted, I realize I haven't been in any public art building for nearly two years. Two years of not experiencing others' creativity—not to mention not producing it. Two years.

I discover a contemporary exhibit by Jenny Holzer. Digital words and phrases scroll up and down impossibly large electronic tubes. I walk among the tubes. It's called *Like Beauty in Flames* and beautiful it is. One word scrolls over and over:

BeAuTy
beAuTy

BEAUTy
beAUty
beaUTY

Something I have always known about myself returns to me as I stand here in this magical space: I thrive on being surrounded by beauty. Without it, my life is meaningless.

This museum reminds me that when art is produced, beauty is created. So for me, sometimes I can immerse myself in beauty by experiencing someone else's art, but mostly I crave the need to produce art so that I can watch the beauty from it emerge. Telling stories onstage makes me extremely happy, because it adds to the beauty of the world. Arriving here today, after seven days of walking the Camino in quiet contemplation, this idea becomes so vividly clear to me.

The pilot light that my friend Guy referenced, the flame that I need so desperately, is the power and passion of beauty. Beauty comes in all forms: people, experiences, and creations. These past seventeen months of not doing theatre, of not crafting ideas and creating worlds, of being locked inside, have not allowed me to create and fill myself up with beauty. Collapsing on the kitchen floor may have been a result of not being able to breathe in any beauty.

Elated with the experience of this space, I need to understand how this place came to be. After rushing to the gift shop, I skim through the history books on the Guggenheim. I discover that, in the 1980s, the city council members of Bilbao were struggling with how to make their city more viable. Much of it was run down, and they needed to fix a decrepit section of the riverfront. Built as a port, this area had become unsafe and deeply unattractive. One wise person suggested that a museum might redefine the area. I try to imagine those meetings:

"What we need is a cultural space—what about a museum?" a wise woman asks.

"Are you nuts? Art? What would that serve?" a man yells.

"We need more industry!" says another angry opponent. Oh, the debates must have been outrageous—and entertaining. Art and beauty to save and revitalize a city? So bold and so unusual. Enter Frank Gehry. I imagine he scribbled some images on a napkin, passed it to a wise person who saw the future in his scratchings, and the rest is history—well, the rest is a stunning museum.

The building was inaugurated in October 1997. While it does have its detractors, it also is credited with revitalizing the city of Bilbao. As a Canadian, I've always known of Gehry's work and have admired the audacity of his images and thinking. Being here makes me beam with Canadian pride. Artists and architects can change the world with their visions. And when we share our artists in a border-free way and allow them to play in each other's sandboxes, we invite a higher level of human interaction, imagination, and innovation. Brilliant things are created.

After the day spent inside, I go out to the front of the museum to digest what I have seen. Suddenly an impressive burst of fog starts spewing out and over the large pond directly in front of the museum. Everyone rushes to take out their phones and record themselves in the fog. It turns out that every hour, for eight wonderful minutes, this mist is emitted over the pond. The weather patterns today are unsettled—changing from rain to sun to cloud to wind. This means that the effect of the fog is uncontrollable and creates various unpredictable patterns. Some people disappear, some people float through. Exactly, I imagine, as Frank Gehry had envisioned it.

While moving about in the mist, I'm feeling awfully thankful to have had a life in the arts. And as an artistic director, I am left with the reminder of how much I like to play and to invite others into creative experiences. I love art and all that it inspires in me and others, as well as in entire communities.

But most of all I am left feeling satiated with beauty and a bone-deep knowing that beauty is why I am here, and what I am supposed to make and uplift in this crazy world.

Today I feel my entire body soar in ways that have been neglected for seventeen months. This intense first week, as I remember the people I've encountered and the ground I've covered, complemented by the art and creativity in Bilbao, has made me incredibly grateful for what is turning out to be a beautiful Camino.

WEEK TWO

INVENTIVE SOLUTIONS

I HAVE A SHORT WALK DEPARTING BILBAO THIS MORNING, SO
I decide it would be swell to get to know the rock more intimately on this leg of the journey. I bring out the little rock that
Bruce gave me, and I place it in my hand. I'll hold it, toss it
about, and keep it close today. There won't be any serious altitude climbing, so it's an excellent time to give the rock a little
bit of sun. This rock reminds me of my family back home enjoying the final days of summer, and although a bit concerned
for them, I am also hopeful that a little one-on-one Papa time
might be just what Abby needs. I take the novel I was going to
read (which I haven't even started) and leave it in the common
room by the front desk, hopeful it will be a welcomed gift for
someone. And that extra water bottle I brought along remains
in the hotel room. I warned them both. I'll greatly appreciate a
slightly lighter bag.

While it is a shorter walk from Bilbao to the riverside
town of Portugalete, it is also one that might challenge my
recently rediscovered love of beauty. I set off knowing it will
be a four-hour hike (the shortest hiking day so far) alongside
the river channel that brings industry into the city through

a commercial boat route. The guidebooks make it tantalizingly clear: I have an option to skip this portion by taking a short twenty-minute high-speed subway ride to the town of Portugalete from Bilbao, as long as I can live with myself for jumping a drab section. I'm committed to walking the entire route, so no skipping sections permitted.

Off I go.

Just north of the downtown area is a series of modern buildings: a shopping mall, a school, and an elaborate sports complex. It's apparent they were all designed and built in the style of the Guggenheim building—with half the money. Poor architects! No doubt some developer said to them, "Design it like that wacky museum so we can be adored as well." A series of quickly imagined and cheaply constructed buildings pays a strange homage to the museum down the road still clearly garnering all the attention. They're just not, well, very nice to look at.

As I walk by possibly every car-repair shop in town, I occasionally encounter a brutalist house or small run-down apartment building, but mostly I see industrial warehouses. It takes me by surprise when I hear laughter coming through an open window, curtains blowing in the wind. People live in these desolate parts? Every thirty minutes it seems a well-dressed senior citizen appears and strolls along as if she is on a fashion runway in Madrid. One woman carries a gift bag—tied with a silver bow. Where she came from and where she is going are mysteries to me. These people aren't walking somewhere through this burnt-out/abandoned/industrial wasteland to celebrate something, are they? It all feels a bit like backstage—actors getting ready in their dressing rooms, moving about through all the stored scenery, ready to bounce onto the stage right on cue.

Approaching the Vizcaya Bridge, which spans the river channel and connects the side I'm walking to Portugalete, I'm stumped by how the bridge actually works. It is no ordinary "bridge." It looks like a gigantic metal arch, made so high that boat traffic can operate nonstop. However, it's a puzzle to me how humans cross. And I do need to get to the other side to continue on the Camino.

As I get closer, I notice the darndest thing—a sort of gondola or floating platform is being pulled across, from high above, by a series of wires that must be at least 150 feet long. The crossing is at sea level, and the method of transport is on a suspended platform. As I approach, I notice it holds about fifty people standing, with room for ten cars. Astonishing. I learn that this mode of transport dates back over a hundred years and, in a two-minute crossing, manages to keep the passageway open to boats at a moment's notice. This becomes the most enjoyable forty-five cents I have ever spent.

I stay at a hotel located beside this amazing bridge contraption and look out my window frequently as the sun sets, to ensure that what I experienced wasn't a mirage. It turns out that the crossing operates around the clock. A day that started as a rather unsightly walk finishes impressively with an inventive bridge—the ingenuity of humans to solve problems in beautiful ways. The little rock agrees.

FEEL LIKE A SWIM YET?

WALKING OUT OF PORTUGALETE begins by gliding upward on a series of outdoor escalators embedded in the middle of an ancient cobblestoned street. It's designed to ease people in their efforts to rise up the hillside effortlessly. Clearly, creative minds are infectious in this town. And my weary feet are grateful for the reprieve.

Early this morning I notice a young couple walking ahead of me. I see bedrolls on their backpacks and make out the lovely sound of French being spoken. That said, I'm determined to walk alone today, since I had quite enjoyed yesterday in solitude with my thoughts. Dreaded pilgrims! They stop to adjust their shoes.

Faking interest with my best *"buen Camino,"* I add a *"¿cómo estás?"*

I'm not actually curious to know the answer; I just think I better play the role of a pilgrim, as insincere as it might be. At this point I notice that the young man has spiked blonde hair and the young woman has a lip piercing (both probably too cool to acknowledge me). Although I expect a grumpy, insincere response, their faces light up as they switch to English (complete with adorable accents), and they show real interest by answering my questions. I stumble for a second at their instant attentiveness and throw in "I will see you at the beach—it's five minutes away," thinking that will be the best way to finish this. They nod in agreement.

Onward I walk, alone again, and shortly arrive at the small beach, which is already packed with families, an impressive accomplishment for nine in the morning. I stop for a *café con leche* and a traditional Spanish offering of a *tortilla* made of egg, cheese, and potato. It's delicious. Returning to an ocean-view walk today feels like a true gift. As I take my second bite of cheesy potato goodness, I look up and discover the French couple walking directly toward me. What to do? As they approach, we begin that awkward dating conversation: "Hello again. Are you stopping for breakfast?" "We might swim first." "Got it." "Well, maybe we should eat now?" A minute later I invite them to sit with me at my table. This day has taken a turn. Why do I do this? Encourage strangers? I seem to be unable to control myself.

Now I'm having breakfast with two kids from Paris who are twenty-five years younger than me. Their gorgeous French-infused accents are intoxicating. We converse easily. They share with me that they are only allowed ten days off work and so have decided to come to Spain and hike the middle of the Camino del Norte. It's not a spiritual journey for them, more like a cheap holiday in the great outdoors.

After breakfast, they want to dip into the ocean, so I offer to watch their bags while they do so. It feels like a nice dad thing to offer. I watch them play in the water—hugging, laughing, and plunging each other under the water joyfully. Observing them, I'm content to allow the day to unfold as it wants to. After they dry off and repack their things, we begin walking together along the ocean on a beautiful sun-filled day.

When I meet a new person, one of my primary concerns

is that they are aware up front that I'm gay. I continue to have an irrational fear that when someone discovers this truth, they will run screaming from me. Better get it over with—and certainly with these two, the sooner the better, I tell myself. I drop the "H bomb" rather quickly. "H" as in "husband." If anything will get them, it will be that. He's married? To a man? I drop the bomb.

"Yeh, my husband is a hiker too, but he really wanted me to walk the Camino alone."

I wait.

I watch.

Nothing happens.

Not even a flinch of an eye.

Ok then.

A sense of relief overcomes me.

I discover their names: Marie and Nicolas—Nicos for short.

Adorable.

We continue walking.

We're joking and goofing around together quite easily. Pretty soon we come up with a ludicrous premise that the two of them are hosts secretly filming a reality show—and that I'm the unknowing guest. Marie is very quick witted and jumps at my silly, silly comments. We are improvising together easily. She creates the idea that the hundred people on the beach where we just spent time are actually all extras in this reality show. And that the goal of this TV show is simple: to get me to swim with them. If they can convince me to jump in the ocean, they will win a million dollars. It's up to them to charm and cajole me to swim. Nicos adds that because I offered to watch the bags and not swim, they failed in their first attempt. Those hundred extras are frustrated, trying to figure out how to help. The film shoot isn't going well; the crew are in a panic. Nicos tells me that he has a monitor in his ear and the producers aren't happy. And so, as we walk together through the very long day, when we go silent, one of them asks, "Do you feel like a swim yet?" And we burst out laughing. It keeps our feet moving.

As the day progresses, I learn that Nicos and Marie were a couple ten years ago—for one delightful year when they were eighteen years old (remember eighteen?)—but that it didn't last, and now they are simply and wonderfully best friends. Their intimacy together is touching. They certainly behave like a couple as I observe them finishing sentences, sharing food, and holding each other close. Due to the scarcity of beds in the *albergues* this year, they bought a tent upon arrival in Spain. They have been camping secretly and illegally all along the trail at hidden beaches or in forests. I admire their tenacity.

Nicos is small framed and fit, with a devilish grin, and is incredibly outgoing and awfully cute. And he loves to flirt. Marie is easily charming and warm, with hair that cascades stunningly down her back, and is quite gorgeous. She, too, loves to flirt. It's all a bit surprising but utterly uplifting. I flirt right back—with both of them. It makes no sense, but I enjoy every sexy minute of it. Only one thing confuses me: what is attractive about someone in their fifties to these French kids?

We arrive at Castro Urdiales and discover a bustling seaside resort town. The ocean dominates the landscape in a stunning way: hundreds of people are all finding their little piece of beach and sun. I've slid into holiday mode, it seems—a holiday with my old friends Nicos and Marie. The only odd image to anyone observing would be the three of us walking across the beach loaded down with our bags, sweaty clothes, and hiking poles—while all the Spaniards around us are sunning themselves, wearing the smallest of swimsuits.

Our nine-hour hike together is finished off with, appropriately, a swim.

We agree to split the million dollars three ways.

On the beach, we set up our towels, change into our swim-suits, and run into the ocean. I'm playing in the waves with my two best friends, feeling utterly comfortable and not the least self-conscious that I'm twenty-five years older (have I mentioned that?) and that I'm crushing on both of them. It is all very, very good.

We find a bar and feast on small, dry sandwiches, *tortillas*, and beer. While sharing everything on the platter of *tapas*, Nicos reveals more to me about their colourful lives. They are both bisexual and feel free to be with anyone they are at-tracted to. They date both sexes and find that they don't have a preference (I had to ask). Trying to act cool, feigning to be sexually knowledgeable and worldly, I take in all of this deli-cious conversation. I'm in awe of their openness: Is it a French thing? An age thing? I don't know. I certainly don't have what they have. But since they have opened up to me, I feel more at ease. I pepper them with questions, and they answer candidly. I think I ask, "How does that work?" more than a few times. I drill them for specifics: When? Where? Why? We laugh, we blush. The level of disclosure and honesty around the table is deeply personal, wildly sexy, and spoken truthfully. It is a wicked testament to the Camino. We all feel safe to express our innermost thoughts.

It's nine in the evening now. Formal restaurants begin to open. Tourists emerge from their hotels, having cleaned off the sand from the day, and families are dressed in their sum-mer finest. An elegant sunset promenade has begun. The three of us have been together for twelve hours now—a hell of a long time to have a first date. We can't stay out any longer because the Parisians need to go on ahead to find a secluded place to camp before nightfall. We make no official plans to reconnect.

"I hope we see you down the road, Dennis," Marie tells me in her beautiful broken English. "I like that we meet you. And have the day today."

They walk toward the sea and disappear into the crowds of hungry tourists now racing to fill the vacant seaside tables. I love the thought of them pitching their tiny tent in the forest somewhere up ahead. I walk to my *albergue*—not knowing if I will ever see them again. And not knowing who is feeling what about whom.

But enjoying the sensations and feelings enormously.

TEAM DENNIS

A QUIET SOLO HIKE BEGINS THE MORNING on this ninth day of walking, as I head toward Laredo, another beach town thirty kilometres away. I love walking directly across the sandy beach as I head west. The landscape undulates gently. This is a peaceful, easy start to the day. I look for my friends occasionally but trust in the Camino to provide: if it is meant to be, it is meant to be.

Meeting the French couple yesterday stirred me up. I didn't sleep very well last night. I can't stop thinking about sex—my relation to it, that is.

I finally admitted to myself that I'm gay at the age of twenty-one. Until then I had experimented/wondered/confused myself. And I waited until the age of twenty-five to come out to my family. A curious notion: to come out. The phrase relates to coming out of the closet—out of hiding, I guess. I came out in the early 1990s, when homosexuality was still not talked about or publicly accepted. But at least it wasn't illegal anymore. Throughout my life, I have always said, "It was easy enough growing up gay"; or, "I never got picked on for being gay"; or, "I have always been accepted." That's not actually true. The reality is that I have managed the path very well and have insisted on living the life I desired to live. But I've been lying about how easy it has been.

The realization that something was unresolved began to surface while on a walk this past spring with my work partner Deb. The pandemic has had an incredibly positive effect on our relationship, bringing us closer together, partially related to converting our work meetings to "walk and talks" where we go for long walks together. Two geese started to squawk at us as we walked past them by the Thames River. All of a sudden, on this particular spring morning, I started on a rant. Once I began, I couldn't stop. It sounded something like this:

"You know what, Deb, I've been lying to myself. Growing up gay in the 1980s and 1990s wasn't easy. It wasn't smooth. I always felt like I had a dirty secret. That I was doing something wrong. I had tried kissing girls and sort of liked it. But it didn't feel right. And I remember thinking while kissing a boy for the very first time, he's going to hate me tomorrow. And that's exactly what he did. He was overwhelmed with shame and ignored me in the school halls for a month. Until, of course, we repeated it all four weeks later. Then there was the time when I was still experimenting, and I had an encounter with a man a few years older than me, and it scared me so much I ran to church the next day in horror. I prayed to God and accepted my fate: I decided, without seeking advice or clarity from anyone, that I was asexual. I would never love anyone because kissing girls and kissing boys felt wrong, for different reasons. I walked through this shame alone. . . . Hmmmm. I think I better work on that." I laughed out loud to Deb, my rant complete.

"You will," she said. "When you have more time to think. You like to walk. I bet you'll process it all one day on a long stroll." Could Deb see into the future?

◆ ◆ ◆

ONCE I CAME OUT TO MYSELF, the shame decreased considerably.

Enter Ken.

I was at a party at the Banff School of Fine Arts, now twenty-one years old, when a handsome young man who played the French horn walked across the room and introduced himself. "Hi. I'm Ken. I think we belong to the same club," he said, his blue eyes gleaming. It was code. He raised a glass of champagne. I raised mine. No one had ever approached me with such directness and confidence before. I was breathless. A few days later, we were kissing unapologetically. In his arms, it felt so perfect and right. It was a sweet, short romance, in which my shameful existence turned beautiful. Thanks to Ken, clarity shot through me like an electric jolt of energy: the music began as the orchestra played, and Ken was the conductor.

After years of wondering, I now knew who I was.

A few years later, I was dating a man named Gavin. I was twenty-five years old, a good son, and yet still lying to my family, telling them that I was single, when in reality I had a boyfriend. I hated lying and so eventually summoned the courage to come out. I wasn't brave enough to make a phone call. I wrote letters: one to each of my four siblings and one to my mom. My dad had passed away when I was twenty-one, not knowing (or did he?) my deep secret. I wrote those five "coming-out letters" and walked to the street corner with my hands shaking. I opened the mailbox, tossed them in, and knew that my fate was sealed. I left it to my family to respond. My siblings each called me when they received the letters and thanked me for sharing this with them. They all said they suspected all along (of course!) but added that they accepted me for who I was.

I had mailed the letter to my mom so that it would arrive at her house a few days before a planned visit. I wanted her to have some time to process the news before seeing me. As she walked toward me at the Vancouver Airport, with tears in her eyes, her first words were, "You're my son. I love you." She asked a lot of questions, as she had never given this any thought before. Her only regret was that she thought I'd have made a terrific priest.

She accepted Gavin with grace. By the end of the weeklong visit, the two of them were singing show tunes together at her request. I listened to my two favourite people belt out "some enchanted evening" together in the front of the car, while I beamed with pride from the back seat. Gavin Crawford has gone on to become one of Canada's funniest comedians—out, proud, and hilarious. I'm grateful for how he helped bridge this relationship. He made a positive and delightful impression on my mom. She grew to adore him as I had—and together we exited that closet I was hiding in.

Last month, just a few weeks before I departed for Spain, my sister Cindy pulled out an envelope and held it up. "Guess what this is?" she said with a sweet twinkle in her eye. A twenty-eight-year-old letter! She didn't know how serendipitous her timing was: I asked her if I could borrow it. It's in my knapsack, unread. I don't remember exactly what I wrote, but when I'm ready, I will read it here on the Camino. I hope it's honest and clever and a bit sassy—this "coming-out letter." After receiving this from my sister, it occurred to me that coming out in the world has put a great responsibility and pressure on the people around me. It's my story, but it's also my family's story.

I hadn't imagined all those memories would reemerge.

I'm starting to notice that the silence of the Camino is a gift and a threat.

I have no one to listen to but myself.

ROUNDING A CORNER FOUR HOURS INTO MY WALK on this very hot day, I see Nicos and Marie resting at a picnic table. I sneak up and, upon realizing it's me, they scream with gales of laughter. While hugging Marie, she tells me "I have missed you today" with such honesty I'm speechless.

I blush.

We walk together.

We chatter.

We share.

We laugh.

We stop at a restaurant packed with Spaniards enjoying a rather fancy Sunday brunch. The host reluctantly finds space for us—three sweaty hikers are not exactly their clientele. Nicos charms our way in. The burger I digest is worth the fight to get seated: sweet, salty, and with a bit of a crunch.

After lunch, we return to the trail, the afternoon heat beating down on us. In the distance up ahead, I see someone familiar, and I get very excited: I know that woman resting on the ground. It's Joy! She's lying on a blanket, sleeping just off the side of the road. After the initial shock of seeing her (it's been more than a week without communication), I introduce everyone. Nicos (again with the great accent) says, "Clearly, Dennis is a magnet for friends."

I ask for a group selfie and Joy shouts, "Team Dennis!"

My heart leaps.

This small band of characters has been doing wonders for me, quietly (and now loudly) cheering me on since we've met. I'm acting casual and light, but it's not what I'm feeling inside. Throughout my time with these people, our dialogue has focused on bigger life questions, not about work, not about careers, and not about politics. Just about the trials and tribulations of everyday life. This trio has nothing to do with my profession, nothing to gain—only friendship. I accept the notion of "Team Dennis" with great humility. We decide to walk on together as a foursome.

As we reach our walking goal for the day, after many more hours in the scorching sun, the French couple head off to a small, secluded beach that they've heard about, where they hope to secretly camp for the night near the ocean. Joy and I head to the town of Laredo and decide to have an impromptu dinner again, to celebrate our unplanned reunion. New relationships are tricky to navigate. But shortly into the evening, Joy and I settle into our friendship, and I can sense that a real bond has indeed formed.

We are a fine pair—Joy and I: being around the same age makes for shared understandings. After a few glasses of wine, she says, "Why are all my friends gay men? I love you guys. But I'd love to meet a straight man—just one."

"But Joy, you know gay men are more reliable and adorable."

"Yes, of course. It's always the way."

I tell her that I was going out of my way to avoid her the day we met—I wanted to walk solo. Bursting out laughing, she admits, "That's what I was doing. I thought I would prefer to walk alone, but it wasn't meant to be."

Joy is very supportive in listening to my parenting woes. A mother of two boys, she says she prayed she wouldn't be pregnant with a girl and was relieved when her prayers came through. She loves her boys. I tell Joy all about my adventures at the Bilbao museum and how it excited me. She understands me instantly.

"What do you hear when I say the word 'beauty'?" I ask Joy.

"A smile. The most beautiful thing in the world is a smile," Joy says, lighting up as the words are spoken. "A smile makes people feel good. And it's so easy to do—and it causes beauty."

Warming up to her subject, she launches in: "On the Camino, I've found that people will share their beautiful selves with you. You just don't feel that in life back home. Here we get on. What works so well is that we are dressed alike—all hikers." She starts to laugh. "You can't tell the bankers from the dreamers from the artists. . . . We all look the same in our sweaty clothes. And here people are accepted for who they are, not for who they portray. You can't hide or put on an act. There is no judgment."

I'm about to throw in a comment, but I can't get a word in. Clearly, she loves this subject. Joy continues, barely taking a breath: "On the Camino, you don't have to act, just be yourself. And you'll see the beauty in walking and nature. Not being in the city. Having time for yourself. Having time. Time is luxury. Taking in blades of grass is the norm here."

I suspect these insights are garnered from Joy walking three Caminos. She concludes, her face all alight, clearly her memories washing over her: "You share and care with everyone. When people actually give a damn about each other . . . you become a different person on your Camino. That's beauty."

And with that we finish our wine in silence, enjoying the insights that we created and shared together. As we say good night, we give each other the biggest hug and promise to find each other down the road.

QUIET

THE NOISE IN MY HEAD has been quieted by the gentle sounds of the ocean throughout this journey. The melodies of waves crashing against the coast, the pounding of the surf . . . soothing distractions. When travelling, I usually find it impossible to shut down completely—my cell phone being too easy to carry around and the notion of checking email "just one time" too tempting. Last summer, in the middle of the pandemic, I found I had become addicted to social media, especially Facebook. So much was happening in the world that I was checking for updates every ten minutes of every waking hour. I didn't want to miss out on the latest comment, accusation, or opinion. I was constantly worried someone was about to write about me. I couldn't stop checking, and it became an obsession. Social media, at its best, is a delightful chance to connect with good friends, where you can share meaningless pictures of your cat, your trip, or your kid's first day of school. I love all that. At its worst, it's a cesspool of useless, biased, and shallow opinions. And I found myself being dragged right into the conversation—always checking for fear of missing out. Realizing that this was adding to my mental exhaustion, I went off Facebook and Twitter completely. It's been over a year, and I haven't been tempted to look. When colleagues update me on the latest gossip, I feel grateful that I have disengaged in this way. I've missed nothing. Shutting it out was vital to help calm the noises in my head.

Not being online for work during my time here in Spain has been a game changer. By this point, I had imagined I'd be worried that everything is happening without me. The opposite has developed. It feels like freedom, an unshackling. The theatre is going on without me, I assume, and I can be present for this experience in front of me.

Here on the Camino, the only way to reconnect with myself has been to embrace all this self-imposed silence. It feels like meditation in a way that I had never understood meditation to work. The extended periods of silence take me deeper inside myself. It's the moments when I don't realize I am so relaxed and open that the thoughts dance in. And even when they arrive, they don't announce themselves—they simply are there. And I suppose that's when the questions begin to form.

For the entirety of this day, I walk alone.

I suspect all my new friends are nearby: the French couple might be somewhere behind, and Joy might be walking just ahead and out of sight. And this day is shorter—a mere five hours of hiking. Easy peasy. I end up at an *albergue* at the eastern edge of the beach in a town called Noja. I eat simply tonight: rather than speaking, I point to a *cerveza* and a cold *tortilla* slice.

Today I do not utter one word out loud to anyone.

LEVEL TEN

LEAVING NOJA ON THE thirteenth day of my journey, I have to catch a tiny commuter boat at the other end of town. The *hospitalario* of my hotel explains to me that it will be a five-kilometre walk down the beach, to where the buildings finally come to an end. Astonishing that a beach could be populated this far and make up the spine of the city. In the distance, I see Joy walking ahead. She must have spent last night here in Noja, I imagine. If I pick up my pace, we will share the boat ride together. I start to walk more quickly but fail to catch up to her, and as I race across the sand to the water's edge, I see Joy on board the small ferry. She is unaware that I'm waving to her. Drat—so close! I've just missed the boat, literally, and consequently Joy. By the time the boat returns for me, Joy will be forty-five minutes ahead down the path—time I'm unlikely to make up.

I cross the river on the ferry, walk through a vibrant little village, and continue to wander the maze that is the Camino del Norte. I marvel at the commitment and effort it takes to create such an obstacle course. I can feel the energy of the people who have walked before me—from ancient times to last

week. I know that it is a constant stream and one to be honoured. I start tapping the yellow arrows along the route with
my hiking pole as I come upon them and say "thank you" out
loud. I don't care who's watching—I'm grateful.

About four hours into my day, a handsome man rushes at
me from behind, sticks waving. He's yelling "heeeeelllllloooo"
as he charges at me. It's Nicos. He gives me a big, awkward
hug: the large backpacks and hiking poles are getting in the
way of fully embracing. Marie appears. I'm surprised that they
have been walking behind me, because by my calculations,
they should be hours in front of me by now.

They fill me in on the previous night's campsite—on a
beach known for nudists. Sadly, they report, mostly older,
out-of-shape men, with the occasional woman, were sunning
about. Marie reports that the clothed women looked embarrassed to be seen with their unfit naked husbands.

We laugh.

We walk.

The talk turns to questions of sex. They go into great detail
about what they will and will not do. The list of things they
will not do is very small. They explain the power of threesomes, and the joy of kissing strangers. Threesomes? With
strangers? Not quite the Camino I had planned. In an effort to
sound cool, I regale them with stories of my youth—the years
before Bruce—and share with them some of the experiences
I've had. But I admit to them that those days are in the past;
I'm monogamous and have been partnered for twenty years.
As I describe all this, Nicos asks me to explain the secret to
my success with Bruce. It's a lovely question. He and Marie
have talked at great length about how Nicos will never find
anyone because he doesn't know how to fully commit to another human. He is afraid to give his heart to someone, Marie
shares. Nicos agrees.

I figured out a few years ago that the more time put into

a relationship, the more levels of "awe" you go through. Like a video game, if you are always starting over, you never get to level ten and the cool area reserved for the experts. Bruce and I are working our way up the levels, and what I'm discovering is that the longer we stay, the higher in levels we go, the more interesting it all is. In short, I hope to grow old with Bruce and discover what that level ten feels like. We're close, but we are not there yet.

I describe the notion of levels to my French companions, all while hiking in the burning sun, and they seem bemused by my offering. I shared my heart. Instead of taking copious notes and pronouncing me brilliant—crickets. No response. Not quite what they want to hear and not something they find useful. So I add, "Just have as much fun and see as much of the world as you can right now. One day you'll meet someone and everything will change." This seems to resonate.

One of the exciting things about the walk to the large urban city of Santander is that you see it come into view a long way off in the distance. It provides hope that the walk ahead may be shorter than imagined. The problem with that is it takes another four hours after you see it to actually arrive. We walk and walk, again through swimmers lounging on the beach and through a very hot residential area, to a boat we need to take to reach the city.

Exhausted, sweaty, and sore, we board the boat for a twenty-five-minute ride that takes us directly into the heart of Santander. We appreciate this rest and enjoy watching the windsurfers, sunbathers, and boaters as we pass. It feels rather extravagant after an exhausting day walking in the heat of the sun.

As the boat nears Santander, Nicos informs us that this city is considered the "contempt" of Spain—not to be admired. Its architecture is bland, and it sports no industry of any interest. It's a terrible introduction and sort of ruins my first impression—another pilgrim telling me what I'm about to experience; however, it becomes apparent that Nicos is absolutely right. Santander is an industrial city without much charm.

After walking into my hostel, I repeat my nightly ritual: a shower to cleanse off the day, followed by hand-washing the most soiled clothing items in need of a rinse. At this point my clothes have stopped bothering to be in the range of "returning to clean and fresh" from merely a bathroom-sink rinse. But I go through the motions. My daily washing is more about ritual than achieving true cleanliness. I must find a laundromat soon.

I join my friends for a seafood dinner comprising freshly caught cod (served as *bacalao al pil pil*) complemented with *cervezas*, outside on a bustling patio. The conversation turns to sex again. There is a pause when Nicos says, "I would like to have sex with two people." Math is not that difficult for me—I can count three people sitting at this table. It feels like a long silence, then I change the subject, my heart racing.

ARE WE THERE YET?

FOR THE MOST PART, THE CICERONE GUIDEBOOK I'm using matches my reactions and experiences closely. And so when the book describes walking out of the large city of Santander to the hilltop village of Santillana del Mar as "excruciating," I beg Marie and Nicos to walk with me. With only two days left on their holiday, they are contemplating skipping this step. Using my reason, logic, and buckets of charm, I suggest that it's vital they walk the path as long as they can and not edit out portions. They succumb to this logic. Marie walks with me today, as Nicos puts earphones in his ears and happily bounces along ahead alone. He disappears rather quickly.

I'm grateful to have a full day walking with Marie. I discover more things that I love about her, mostly her deep empathy and caring. We ask wide-reaching questions today: She says to me, "What do you dream about for your child?" I ask, "How do we know we are making the right choices in our lives?" No question is rushed. We share our personal stories: My parents are deceased, and her father recently passed away. Her relationship with her mother has always been deeply complicated and scarred. When her mother was diagnosed with cancer a few years ago, she admits to me that she felt no sadness. She says it simply but clearly. She misses her dad. The volley of questions and answers is nonstop. Marie is an absolute revelation.

It is, however, an excruciatingly difficult walk to negotiate, as the guidebook warned. In the middle of this day that is projected to take twelve hours on foot in the sweltering sun, the highlight (I use the term ironically) is hiking around a colossal factory compound that continues to spew dirt into the air as we take a few hours to circumnavigate it. I have no idea what we ingest, but it cannot be good. Smoke clouds overwhelm the sky. It's like something out of a science fiction horror movie.

I drop off Marie with Nicos at a hostel just outside of the town of Santillana del Mar after eleven hours of walking. Nicos arrived a remarkable two hours before us, which he credits with listening to Lady Gaga nonstop during his walk. All that dancing and strutting along the path—I'm sure Nicos danced like no one was watching.

My hotel is another hour uphill, in the centre of town, so I carry on alone, exhausted. As I continue to climb toward my bed for the night, getting my legs up the hill becomes overwhelming. Every step is a heroic effort, and the desire to stop constantly overwhelms. The hiking poles help enormously to keep me dragging myself forward. The cars are driving dangerously fast and close to me, but I keep stepping along. I read every street sign, calculate ever kilometre. As I taught my child to say before she learned it herself, I mutter, "Are we there yet, are we there yet, are we there yet?" That annoying chant provides little relief, because I know the answer: *No, we're not there yet; no, we're not there yet; no, we're not there yet.*

I just want to lie down.

Approaching Santillana del Mar, I notice that this hilltop city is covered in glorious cobblestones and is historically intact and breathtakingly serene. This gruelling day is ending on a high, in what appears to be a mirage of an opulent, preserved town. As I walk the streets, I'm amazed to see a world bustling with tourists, the expected stores selling local ham, cheese, wine, and T-shirts. Such a contrast from the majority of my day. Walking through all this history and charm is a novelty for a Canadian. (The next day Marie isn't that impressed: "Come to France—all our towns look like this.") For me, it is the unexpected payoff after a very difficult day of hiking.

I sit in a courtyard, under a tree covered in twinkling lights, eating the grandest meal I would likely have on the Camino. I treat myself to duck confit with a delicious fresh salad. It doesn't take long to feel restored once again. How quick the twelve gruelling hours are forgiven with the delight of discovering this irresistible preserved little town.

JESUS IS FROM PARIS?

THE LAST DAY WITH THE KIDS involves a shorter walk, from Santillana del Mar to Comillas. It's along the ocean, and it is a much easier hike—all things considered. However, today our happy threesome can't find our groove. Partly I think a lot about our sexual conversations, and though I was glad to have them, rather than making me feel like I want to go back in time and be more adventurous (i.e., frolic in a tiny tent on the ocean with two Parisians), they actually do the opposite. I realized over duck confit last night that I am satisfied with this area of my life, and I won't act as if I'm twenty-eight again. I'm interested in new conversations at this point, but Nicos doesn't stop talking about sex today; when he makes a reference regarding a couple passing by that is meant to be sexy but that I find rather vulgar, I raise my voice: "You've crossed the line, Nicos. Can we please stop talking about sex?" He's instantly apologetic and admits he is known for pushing people too far. It's awkward. Silence descends over our trio.

Then Jesus appears.

Seemingly out of nowhere, a man dressed in a long robe, with a full beard and carrying a fabric sack on a stick, appears to us on the trail. He is decidedly not wearing the latest hiking gear, and his sandals seem directly taken from the Bible.

He says hello to us first in Spanish, then in English. We ask him where he is from and are surprised to hear the word "Paris." Jesus is from Paris? That's a revelation. It turns out this man has walked a Camino before but, as we would learn, has decided to do it as authentically as possible this time. He carries no papers, he has no money, and he has no plans for where to stay. He relies on compassion from people on the road. His name is Pierre, and he is grateful to speak French with Marie and Nicos. I follow behind in awe that Jesus has joined us on our journey.

Pierre is likely thirty-five years old and has an extraordinary sense of peace about him, and he does bear a striking resemblance to a certain biblical figure. He walks with us for a few hours. I feel a bit overpacked compared to him—guilty that I'm not walking the way he is—and am in awe of his confident, calm demeanour. I don't doubt that it is exactly the spirit in which the real Jesus would have walked.

Entering a square of a small village, the four of us sit for a rest. A middle-aged woman and her small yappy dog appear. She begins complimenting us pilgrims for being on the way to Santiago. This woman has great energy and joy and only speaks Spanish. When she discovers she's among French companions, she begins to attempt to speak in French. Hearing *"bonjour, comment ça va?"* spoken with a Spanish accent is incredibly adorable. Out of nowhere, a distinguished-looking man in his sixties appears from a different direction. Wearing light cotton slacks, a classically Spanish blue collared shirt, and a stylish straw fedora, he joins in the enthusiastic complimenting. He follows up by offering to buy us all a drink: beer, cola, water—whatever we want. It's such a kind and generous offer to a bunch of strangers. After much prompting, we humbly say yes. The man passes some cash to the woman (I can't decipher what their relationship is, but they seem to be friends). She disappears down the road. Returning a few minutes later with a large bottle of water for me, she then plugs euros into a cola machine on the street for the other three. We thought she worked at the bar—clearly not. These two strangers and the dog are a mystery. I can't figure out their story or where this is all heading.

I've been given something by total strangers because I'm walking as a pilgrim. It's moving and sort of unsettling to be rewarded in this way. This is not how I see myself, receiving water from strangers. When Pierre (Jesus) thanks the man for his generosity, the graceful Spaniard says very gently, "No, no, no. It's normal." A pause descends among our group. Normal. And with that he wishes us a *"buen Camino"* and vanishes. A moment later the woman and her dog wander off in a completely different direction. Were they all a mirage? Our little band isn't quite sure what just happened. We drink our gifts in silence. The phrase "It's normal" to help strangers rings loudly in my ears. If only it was universally true.

I think I officially became a pilgrim today.

After a few quiet minutes of reflection, we decide to walk on—leaving Jesus to continue eating bread that he must have been given on the way. I can't help but wonder what power this man, Pierre, has by trusting that the world will provide. For clearly there is a power here.

The rest of the walk is filled with gentle conversations. Dinner is quiet with Nicos and Marie—we feign lightness and silliness, but we know our time together is ending soon. Our sadness overwhelms our joy. When we finally say our goodbyes, we have tears in our eyes. It is incredibly sad to think that we will not walk together anymore. They have become my best friends on this Camino. We exchange email addresses, and I make a promise to come to France as soon as possible. They guarantee me an insider's tour of Paris.

I fell in love with these two. I'm deeply grateful for their openness and willingness to spend these honest days with me. They have to go to work as soon as they get back to Paris—apparently, Marie for a prominent magazine and Nicos for an important international trading company. I don't really know what they do; we never talked about work. We talked about love, about living, about joyful things. On one level, it feels like we didn't finish some of our conversations, and on another level, it felt so right that it would stay like that. They were so completely connected to me—and I to them. So we did have a threesome after all. Just not in the way any of us might have imagined.

Today I met Jesus, said a teary goodbye, and became a pilgrim.

WEEK THREE

THE RIGHT THING TO DO

I WAKE UP IN A TIDY HOSTEL in a room with ten bunks. I'm used to this communal routine now. And I am grateful to have a typical Camino experience such as this. I'm feeling more comfortable sleeping among others and quietly and efficiently pack without disturbing anyone. I head out the door.

With my friends on a train back to Paris, I'm decidedly alone once again. As I walk out of town, on this sixteenth day, I feel the Camino as a soloist. It's up to me and only me to make this journey ahead. There is a sense of changing gears to kick-start the day: can't rely on someone else to order lunch, must watch way markings closely. No one to second-guess the choices made. It's the blessing and curse of solo walking. More than anything, it provides more reflective time to listen to the voices in my head.

I arrive in the town of Unquera. In all of my detailed planning, I wasn't able to secure a place to sleep in the town of Colombres, just ten minutes beyond and across a pretty river, known for its well-preserved architecture. When Colombres sells out, people stay in Unquera—the runner-up. And that's where I will stay tonight.

By the look of the hotel on the internet, it is going to be a dated, badly rated, dull night in an ugly town. I haven't been looking forward to this stop. But I couldn't figure out how to plan my way to something more interesting. As I walk into town, I notice it's one long street of shops. Just barely out of sight is the highway and in the distance is a river keeping me from the pretty town of Colombres. I lower the bar and decide that Unquera will be a useful refuelling stop. It's good to just have extra rest sometimes. After settling into my hotel room, with a view of a garbage dumpster and cars and a ghastly painting on the wall of a generic mountain range, I search for a pharmacy. For the past few days, I've been having stomach troubles and think I better stock up in case of an emergency. It's not something I want to talk about at the best of times, so I hope I will find a remedy fast and get out quickly. Looking through every box of medicine on the shelves of the stylish *farmacia* without success, I realize I will be forced to ask someone for help. I approach the counter and an uninterested and distracted woman stares back at me. After confirming she doesn't speak English, I simply say "diarrhea." I had looked it up and the word is remarkably close in Spanish. I feel confident. She draws a blank face. I pull out my phone, my humility descending, and I lift the screen to her, the Spanish word for diarrhea on full display: *"diarrea."* Suddenly it all makes sense to her. Without moving from behind the counter, she lowers her hand, while still keeping eye contact, and magically pulls out a box from just out of site, without even looking down—as if she does this gesture ten times a day. No reaction. Just a box. I pay and leave quickly.

Siestas are a real thing in Spain and, from three in the afternoon to eight in the early evening, I've come to expect everything to be closed. But just as the sun is beginning to set, I know the town will become alive and bustling. Clothing stores, shoe shops, and bakeries are all actively open and in full force. Back home, shops would be closed, and the restaurants would have been serving dinner for hours by now. As I stroll down this one-street wonder just after eight, I see an open barbershop. Desperate to have my hair cut, I bounce in. This barber is leathery skinned, fully moustached, and looks like he's been in the hair-cutting business for centuries. I'm not prepared with the words for "cut my hair," so the barber looks at me in utter confusion. Which makes no sense, because why else would I be in a barbershop but to get my hair cut? I use my fingers as scissors—my mime skills kicking in. He looks utterly lost. What could I possibly be wanting from him in this barbershop? Seriously. Not taking "I don't understand you" for an answer, I carry on cutting my whole head with my imaginary finger scissors. What does he think I'm asking? To go out dancing with me? What is the square root of . . . ? What???? Eventually he asks, *"¿Quieres un corte de pelo?"* And I shout out, "Yes! Cut *(corte)* my hair *(pelo)*!" With a shrug, he has me sit. It's then I realize the background noise is not a television set; the sound is coming from his cell phone playing a live tennis match. I'm interrupting his game. He proceeds to stare at it for four minutes before cutting my hair. And during my haircut—when the crowd starts to scream—he stops cutting and goes over to his phone. No apologies. What I do notice when he does spare the time to cut my hair is that he is likely a master barber—his technique is methodical and precise. When I go to pay, I'm one euro short in cash. After a grumpy shrug, he indicates the ten euros I have given him will be enough.

I head back directly to my hotel to collect some coins. It's only one euro, but I'm not going to pay him less than he asked. I think of Yogi.

We didn't have much money growing up. My mom would take a calculator when she went to the grocery store and add up the cost of the items as she put them in her cart. She wanted to ensure she had enough money. Sometimes, after pulling her cart for the twenty minutes it took to get home, she would realize that the store had double charged her for an item. She'd then walk back to the store to ask for her three dollars back. She would show the receipt, and they would refund her the money. I vividly remember one time when Mom arrived home and, while double-checking the groceries in the cart, became very upset. This time they had forgotten to charge her for a five-dollar item. This wasn't right. So she walked back and willingly gave them the money owed. "Of course, that's the right thing to do," Yogi told me later.

When I return to the shop, the barber is shocked to see me. I place one euro on the counter, and he says quite loudly, "No!" Is his pride hurt? I insist and walk away as fast as I can without further discussion. It is his money. And an excellent haircut. And that is what Yogi would have done.

Sitting in the centre of this tiny town of Unquera, I'm showing off my new hair to Spaniards who look my way, eating macaroni with chorizo and tomato sauce, complemented with *patatas bravas*. It was not predicted: gratitude for this little town that isn't the other, prettier one down the road.

A DAY IN THIS LIFE

WHILE ENJOYING MY DINNER in the square, I make note of my daily routine:

Morning awake.
Creaky bones.
Pack bag with great focus.
Nervous moment leaving the security of the hotel.
The unknown of today's walk.
Step outside.
First hour the best.
Silence and dark.
Morning thoughts flow.
Bones relax: motion is lotion.
Excited about a little break.
Improvised lunch.
Always take off shoes midday.
Get as much walking covered before the sun is at its peak.
Hard to get going after lunch.
Counting the steps begins.
Checking the app for location.

Checking the app too often.

Last two hours are the most challenging, no matter what.

Sweating out of every pore, soaking all clothes.

All attempts at cleanliness gone.

Checking in and showering off the day.

Unpack contents of Gregory all over the room.

Clothes everywhere.

Magically, all restored—exhaustion of day forgiven.

Rest and review day.

Sightsee.

Decide between:

1. Bar-service food.
2. Staying up late for dinner.
3. Picnic on bed.

Mostly in bed by nine.

Exhausted.

Fall asleep with grin on face.

IT WAS MY JOB

STARTING OUT EARLY IN THE MORNING is an exhilarating feeling: packing Gregory in silence, leaving the key in the door as I close it quietly, going out the front door. I hear a rooster, but see no one on the streets. The sun begins to rise as if to light my way on this, my seventeenth, day.

Walking out of Unquera, I cross an ancient bridge spanning a vibrantly blue–coloured river glistening in the morning light. Immediately after, I head directly up a steep hill, my poles and body instantly put to the hiking test, and the seven-in-the-morning sweating begins, while every step opens up a view of the surrounding mountains and hills. I see morning fog settling in the valley all around me. These puffy balls of clouds are being cradled inside the undulating formation of the hills.

After a few minutes, I walk into the fabled town of Colombres. Its architecture is a marvel—each *casa* created with the greatest of care. The town square is preserved as if it was built last year. Pride of ownership is evident: all gardens are trimmed with precision. I would have enjoyed staying here last night (except then I wouldn't have this fine haircut, now would I?). Colombres is one of those towns that people fanta-size about retiring to. It's surely a second home to many people who escape here on weekends from Madrid or who travel here from Barcelona for the summer. I make a note in my journal to learn more about this place, which is code for study the real estate and imagine moving here soon.

I FIRST HAD THE EXPERIENCE of wanting to live abroad when I was thirty-four and was invited to visit the celebrated author Timothy Findley in the south of France. For a glorious week in springtime, Bruce and I were welcomed into the winter home of Findley and his partner, Bill Whitehead.

Findley was one of the great Canadian authors, with such acclaimed novels as *Not Wanted on the Voyage*, *Pilgrim*, and *The Wars*. He accomplished many things in his career: besides being a novelist, he was a playwright and actor too. He was revered. And nearly forty years my senior. After I directed a successful reading of a play at the Stratford Festival in 2000, I received a call from the artistic director, Richard Monette, inviting me to transform Findley's radio drama *The Trials of Ezra Pound* into a stage play for the following season. Findley would be available for rewrites and would attend rehearsals. I was terrified at the prospect of working with this renowned writer. After calming myself down, I got to work. Since Findley and Whitehead spent winters in France, my first connection to them was through the fax machine. I sent Findley a six-page fax with all my suggested changes for the production. I began: "Dear Mr. Findley, It is a pleasure to meet you. . . ." I didn't have the guts to pick up the phone. A few days later a fax arrived for me. The letter was very supportive of my suggestions. I could breathe again. It finished with: "And Dennis, please call me Tiff."

The first time I actually met Tiff in person was a few months later—the day before rehearsals began. Over a long and booze-filled lunch, we talked about the play and our lives.

He told me how excited he was that I was the director. He couldn't say enough kind things. I went to the washroom after sharing our second bottle of wine and talked aloud to the mirror: "He likes me. It's going to be ok."

Rehearsing *Ezra Pound* was one of the happiest and most fulfilling experiences of my life. The cast was led by the incredibly charming and versatile actor David Fox, and I had hired an ensemble of truly talented, kind souls who were up for the challenge of staging the ideas that I presented to them. Tiff and Bill attended most rehearsals.

On one particular day, I was trying to stage a moment that was important to me. I wanted everyone in the cast to exit quickly, the large doors swinging shut and the stage emptying to a great silence. I rehearsed it over and over. People started to lose patience with me. I worried that Tiff was thinking, *Get on with saying my words.* I begged the cast, "One more time, please." Everyone threw themselves into it, and the last time, it finally worked. My first reaction was to spin my body around to see Tiff's reaction. He had his hands held to his face, his eyes were lit up, and I could see he had just inhaled—the way you do when you are left breathless. I'll remember that moment forever.

The show was well received. Later that fall the artistic director called again. This time he wanted me to direct a large family spectacle on the Avon Theatre stage, *The Scarlet Pimpernel.* Then he added, "Oh, and Tiff wants you too. To direct a new play he's writing called *Shadows*, which will be part of the inaugural season of the new Studio Theatre." I was thrilled. "He'll be spending the winter in France, of course, and they want to work with you in person on this, so they have offered to fly you over. And you will stay with them." Jaw drop.

Early that winter, a month before they escaped for the warmth of France, Bruce and I had a delicious dinner with them in Stratford, snow falling heavily as we dined.

"Were you actually excited that you had a young, basically unknown director assigned to your show?" I asked.

"No. I wasn't. I actually was disappointed. And a bit mad," Tiff said. I started to laugh. Having confessed easily to me, he joined in the laughter with his characteristically intoxicating loud roar.

"I wondered why I wasn't offered an experienced director—just you," he concluded.

"Then why did you say all those incredibly kind things to me the day before rehearsals?" I asked.

"You were my director. It was my job to inspire you and support you. I had to make sure you were confident. That was my job."

"Right! Now I understand. I had a funny feeling!" I yelled out. "I didn't figure it out in the moment, but as I've gotten to know you better and we've become friends, looking back I thought something didn't quite add up."

We were all laughing at this point.

But then Tiff added, "Look how it turned out."

We arrived in Provence, in the lesser-known village of Cotignac, France, a few months later. Their property was humble and perfect, with a view of the valley and surrounding orchards. They had converted the garage into Tiff's study where every morning he would write. They would have lunch on the patio overlooking the rolling hills and vineyards. Over wine, Bill would read out loud the words that Tiff had handwritten that morning. The two of them would edit. That afternoon, Bill would type up the script while Tiff would nap. This was their life in Provence.

By this point, though, Tiff had developed an illness that was slowing him down and would eventually require him to go into the hospital. Bill managed to provide us with a thoroughly detailed, insightful, and personal tour of Provence in our week together. We stocked up on rosé at the local *magasin de vin,* and I enjoyed my first ever duck confit at a tiny four-table restaurant tucked behind a church that was known only to the locals.

We worked on *Shadows,* but Tiff's health was quickly declining, and he became the major focus of our visit instead. A month later, back in Canada, Bill called. Tiff had passed away. He added, "Tiff loved you."

That summer we produced his play at Stratford without him. Nothing about the production was right. The incredible actor Brent Carver, Tiff's friend as well, was starring in it. For many of us, it simply was too sad. The play came and went. It was not particularly good, and the direction was distracted at best.

A relatively new friendship was taken from me too quickly.

A year after Tiff had died, Bill published Tiff's journal of his personal notes. It's called *Journeyman: Travels of a Writer.* I came upon this entry on page sixty-four: "I began the first draft of *Shadows.* . . . I have Brent Carver, my God!!! And I'm hoping for Dennis Garnhum as director. I'm the luckiest man in the world. Period."

I'M STANDING HERE IN the town square of Colombres, Spain, on a warm summer's morning in the middle of week three, about halfway through walking my Camino. But emotionally and mentally right now, I'm transported back twenty years ago in time: to a place of fearless creativity, to being exposed to the possibility of exotic travel, under the supportive guidance of a mentor who allowed the artist inside me to soar. I'm taken to many places all at once: to France, drinking rosé with Bruce and Bill; onstage in Stratford, explaining a direction to David Fox; but mostly to the rehearsal hall, and Tiff's energizing eyes shooting rays of encouragement straight to me.

Digesting all of this, I put my hands to my face, my eyes light up, and I inhale a deep breath. It's as if I am gathering dormant pieces of my past and reviving them—reminding myself how they've shaped me and how hard I've worked to claim the creative life I've lived.

My memories inspire me forward.

BLURRY

FOR THE NEXT FEW DAYS, the journey becomes a bit of a blur.

In Llanes I am excited about the accommodation that I have booked: I will be staying at the Albergue La Casona del Peregrino. It looked like a place that would be filled with pilgrims—or, at least, that is what the name suggested.

After a hearty welcome by a warm couple, the *hospitalario* asks, "*¿Que tal?*" To which I offer, "*Cansado!*" (Tired!) We laugh together. "Normal," they both agree. I'm told to follow the husband to my room in the garden. The garden? Sounds incredible. As we descend the front steps of the *albergue* and make our way to the back, the garden looks more like a motel strip—complete with cars. I count six rooms that were probably added in the 1970s. I won't be staying in the main building communally with others, it seems. I will be in the motel and quite alone.

Llanes is a fashionable town with a small beach (too windy, too cool today to get in the ocean though—I tried, feebly) and a vibrant town centre around the marina. It's a small town with no traffic lights and just a few meandering seaside cobblestoned streets. Tonight I'm too tired to take it in, though, and feeling guilty about it. I wander around the marina observing the pretty people and their adorable children, exhausted, so I go to bed early. I hear people on the streets gathering to party as I doze off.

Heading out in the morning, I hope for a better state of mind as I hike toward the town of Ribadesella. The walking today takes me around small lakes, and I notice one particularly cute church with a tall steeple. I'm behind on my stamp collecting and need to get in the habit more. The last one hundred kilometres will require two stamps a day to be considered official. I better try harder with the passport.

I approach the church and pull on the handle.

Locked.

No church for me today.

GROWING UP, WE ALWAYS WENT TO MASS EVERY SUNDAY. In our teen years, we didn't like to go at the earlier time prescribed by our parents, to attend as a family. As long as we went to a mass, our mom would relent: we could go on our own. One year my sister Jackie and I agreed to go to the late-morning mass at a different church. Just the two of us. My sister is two years older than I am, and we fought most of the time growing up. But when we spent Sunday mornings together, we got along just fine. That's likely because we would walk right past the church and not go in. Instead, we would carry on three more blocks and slip into the local fast-food restaurant Burger King. We'd order food and spend an hour together. I can't remember who came up with the plan, but I'll point my finger at my sister. Every week, when we got home, mom would ask about mass. We always managed a lovely little lie about our experience. This is the one secret Yogi never knew to her dying day: that my sister and I attended the Church of Burger King every Sunday for a year. I'm not proud of it, but I did appreciate the forced time together that I had with my sister. I enjoyed that she and I were in collusion and on the same side about something for a change.

AFTER MY FAILED ATTEMPT at going to church today, I walk four more hours alongside the ocean and enjoy the sound of the crashing waves, all the way to Ribadesella. This place is a wonder. The large port city has two very different sections. The original section is called the "old town," which dates back to the thirteenth century, and the strange suburban area closer to the ocean is the "new town" and dates back only to the nineteenth century.

It's Sunday and all the guide reports regarding closed shops are for naught. Everything's open and it's essentially business as usual. The day of rest prescribed to Catholics doesn't seem to be in effect here. There's even clothing drying on clotheslines outside, proving that the traditional rules are not being followed. I pass by a church where service is letting out. I debate about going in. I walk on—not feeling inspired to open a letter today.

Through the miracle of WhatsApp technology, I'm able to show off the town to my family back home—this kind of video sharing was unheard of merely a couple of years ago. This is the first time I've seen their faces since leaving Canada. I'm excited to show Abby the market stalls lined up along the harbour. I point out the ice cream vendors. And I ask her opinion on which flavour I should choose. Chocolate. Always chocolate. I can see Bruce and Grandma Helene on my phone, watching from behind her—both supportively smiling at my guidance and narration. Abby gets distracted rather quickly and tells me she has to go. Eleven-year-olds have busy schedules, apparently. But she is in good spirits, so that's what matters most.

I tell Helene that I have been walking softly, which I have discovered to mean many things:

Embrace what comes before me.

Not to rush.

Appreciate silence.

Marvel at surroundings.

Honour my precious feet.

Bruce and I have a light conversation regarding the Camino. We've been emailing intermittently throughout these past three weeks—mostly to reassure Bruce that I'm still alive. There is so much I want to share with him—so many ideas brewing—but, strangely, nothing comes out as a profound pronouncement.

"Any insights this week?" Bruce asks.

"Nothing comprehensible. A bit of this, a bit of that."

"Blurry?"

"Blurry."

"Sounds like you're on track. Over a year of unhappiness isn't likely to be solved in three weeks," Bruce suggests. "But I'm glad you're meeting people and staying healthy."

We say our goodbyes and hang up. I'm glad to see the trio from back home tonight, but I'm reminded of the difference between being on a journey and hearing about a journey. As supportive as my family is, there is only one person here. That's me. And it's far from over. Speaking with them, I may have naively assumed everything is healed and all problems solved. The phone call reminds me I have more work to do in order to figure out my future steps.

I wander the harbour at sunset feeling strangely more alone having had this call. Can it be that I am getting tired of this trip? Will this feeling continue? Too much of a good thing? Homesick? Bored? I know one thing: we won't be likely to use technology to see each other anymore on this trip. It doesn't provide either side the thrill I imagined it might.

As I lie awake in my bed, my phone lights up, and I get a new message on WhatsApp. This one's from Joy. She took a bad tumble back in Comillas and has had to add a couple rest days. She's been hobbling forward with her knee and leg in great pain, so she has been taking her days very slowly. And unless she moves ahead by jumping on a bus, she won't be able to catch up to me. Joy's not very joy filled right now, depressed about her very sore knee. She has to wait and see how quickly it will heal. I text her: "But you'll make it to that church in Santiago eventually, I know it." I was looking forward to seeing her again. Counting on it, actually. Now, it's hard to say if that will ever happen. Joy's Camino seems in jeopardy.

Blurry abounds.

A BEAUTIFUL PLACE

I JOIN THE CAMINO ROUTE this morning as I walk out of the old town in Ribadesella, toward the beach in the new town, in hopes of a *café con leche* before carrying on my journey. I come across a small restaurant with two customers sitting at the window. I'm thrilled to see that they actually have *huevos y tocino* on the menu. It's an homage to North Americans—Spaniards don't eat eggs and bacon for breakfast. Overpriced and delicious, it's perfect. I devour it guiltlessly.

Walking along the ocean after breakfast, I come to Playa de Berbes just outside of the town of Vega, around ten in the morning. I notice a long inviting stretch of beach with very few people on it. I hike across the sand in my hiking boots, not the easiest task, toward the western side. As I walk, I pass a couple of naturalists—with not a tan line to be seen.

I think about stripping off my clothes and jumping into the alluring ocean. I'd like to but I'm nervous. It's not a very Canadian thing to do. I contemplate my options. I find an empty section of beach. I look to my left, I look to my right. No one. I take off my pack, my hiking shirt, and my shorts. I'm about to bare all and run into the water, and I'm in the process

of pulling down my underwear when a family of four appears over a sand dune. I jerk up my underwear and stand frozen. I can't be naked in front of a family with children. How inappropriate would that be? I try to act casual and walk along the water's edge. I behave as if I love to walk around in my underwear on the beach. *Yep, that's what I do. La dee dah.* I don't want to offend anyone. I turn and see the boys taking off their clothes, and I am shocked to see the father and mother undressing as well. And it's an absolutely beautiful sight to behold—the freedom they have in their skin. Inspired by their boldness, I take off my underwear without hesitation, and rather than run into the ocean, I walk softly toward the awaiting waves in my naturalness, for all the world to see. I enjoy the sand beneath my feet, and the cool water on my skin as I immerse myself in the gorgeous, fresh, inviting Atlantic Ocean. They frolic as a family, and I feel both seen and unseen by them. I'm playing in the waves now like a child—letting each wave crash against my naked backside, knocking me into the sea. I'm laughing out loud every time I get pushed over by a wave. They can hear my laughter.

With the sun beating on my back in contrast to the cold brisk water, a sense of freedom envelops me. I'm loving the sensation of my skin in the water—and nothing in between. I walk back to my towel and lie down, unabashedly naked, to take in the rays. The beach begins to fill with other naturalists. After thirty minutes of the sun warming and soothing my skin, I reluctantly begin to pack up. I would love to stay here all day, but the Camino calls. As I dress back into my hiking outfit, I see the boys continuing to play in the sand, and the dad reading a book. I walk on, refreshed.

Farther down the coast, at Playa Arenal de Morís, there is an empty picnic table where I feel compelled to stop. I make my simple lunch: tomatoes and cucumber with a fresh baguette. While I eat, I observe surfers taking lessons in some steep waves and swells. The instructor demonstrates a wicked and dangerous-looking maneuver; the two students imitate and crash into the water. They repeat the action over and over until they catch the wave as the instructor intended.

Farther down the cliffside path, I come upon Playa de La Espasa as I approach the town of La Isla. I walk on quietly, enjoying all the humanity—everyone here playing as they wish, freely, happily, on a sublime Monday afternoon in August. As I carry on to my hotel in Colunga, just outside of La Isla, I think, *Well, that's not a very pilgrimy kind of day, Mr. Garnhum.* I didn't quite expect days like this on the Camino—free of worry or care and bathed in salty air and true pleasure.

In Colunga, after settling into my hotel room, I return to the ocean and find a spot on a bluff with a perfect view. People are starting to gather near me, all eyes to the sea, hoping to catch a performance—the sun setting into the sea. I'm an old soul and a hopeless romantic, so I love a good sunset: it's a beautiful thing.

ABOUT A DECADE AGO, I declared to my friends that "beauty" is my favourite word. I had come to realize that it's my reason for being—to seek out beauty. I wake up and look for beauty (my family, my house, my cup of coffee), spend my day creating beautiful things (staging a play with a roomful of actors, working with a designer to create a set, reading a new play), and finish by ensuring that beauty surrounds me (my family again—now with a glass of wine). It's been my lifelong goal, this constant search for beauty.

I suppose I found my way to beauty as a reaction to my early years surrounded by so much ugly. As the youngest of five, I was born into a family that was already unsettled. My father was an alcoholic. It shaped most of our home life. There was not much beauty to be found. Growing up, I only knew a mother held back by a husband who would come home every night, drink half a case of beer, and then pass out. He wasn't physically abusive. He didn't yell at me. He was a nice enough man, but he was emotionally absent to me. A ghost. My mother was burdened with managing a family of five kids, while trying to play the role of the dutiful Catholic wife. Because of his drinking, my father was unambitious to invoke or inspire family activity. We were left to find our own adventures.

From a very young age, I witnessed a great deal of yelling and fighting among my parents and my older siblings. I learned to become as small as possible and tried to stay quiet and be the "good boy." I avoided confrontation at all costs. I thought the world of my mother and sat up with her many nights in the backyard listening to her stories of growing up in Quebec, which I adored. Her childhood in a French land seemed so exotic and peaceful. And I listened painfully as she told me about the happier days with my father, when they were first courting.

I was twelve years old when Mom confided in me that she thought Dad was drinking her sherry. She drank too, but only a few glasses a week. Nothing substantial. But she began to think the sherry she was drinking was watered down. One evening, a week later, I walked into the kitchen and saw my dad holding her sherry bottle under the sink tap. The water was running. He was refilling the part that he had drunk. We locked eyes and held each other's gaze for what felt like an eternity. I walked away and we never spoke of it. And I couldn't bear to share with Mom what I had seen—it would have caused another uproar.

When I was fourteen, my parents went to my dad's office Christmas party one Saturday night in December. My sister Jackie and I were allowed to stay home alone. My parents left the house at five in the afternoon. At seven, two hours later, we heard someone trying to open the front door. From the sounds we were hearing, we thought someone was trying to break in. We cowered by the back door in tears, prepared to escape. Eventually the door opened. My mom was carrying my dad back into the house. At the Christmas party, he had drunk so much too quickly that he had become incoherent.

We never spoke of it.

The next day the family went to church.

As we did every Sunday.

THIS SCENE AND COUNTLESS OTHERS like it that had come before are the reasons art came to my rescue. Early on I realized I could use theatre to help me escape from my painful surroundings.

The first time I performed a puppet show in my basement, when I was seven years old, with my family watching, was electric. I had designed the sets (curtains on strings), hired the actors (socks on my hands), and wrote the story. It was about two friends: a puppy and a rabbit that got lost in a field. The mom and dad appeared and rescued them, and they celebrated by sharing a chocolate cake (a paper cutout). Sitting in a row of lawn chairs I'd set up in the basement beforehand, my captive audience applauded my efforts.

From then on, I realized "pretend problems" in plays were more fun to be around than the real ones at home.

All these decades later, my spirit still soars when I direct. It allows me to live in a beautiful place. That's the power that art has always had on me: an uncontrollable pull, a desire and an essential need to create and to escape to beauty. And by being the director, I suppose, I also have a greater chance to influence and control the stories I surround myself with. That's something I couldn't achieve at home growing up.

I SHAKE MY HEAD and remind myself to be present: You're here on the bluff. The sun is setting. Take it in. As the sun continues to lower over the ocean, the dark colours of the sea in the waning light start to dominate the water. In these magic few minutes, the intense colours dance together and reveal, sometimes for mere seconds, dark new patterns and shadows.

The colours capture my imagination.

MY PROCESS FOR DIRECTING PLAYS begins with the same impulse every time. I didn't know it at the time, but even while directing in elementary school, I was asking myself, *How does this story improve the world? How can I ensure that more beauty is created as a result of this production?* I have to fall madly in love with a play the first time I read it in order to want to direct it. I hold that first impression sacred. I'm usually vibrating with excitement—I've never understood the physiological reason why this happens, but it takes over my whole being. My heart races, my body shakes. I'm taken away from the troubles of my day, my situation, or my worries.

It's obvious that most musicals and comedies provide joy, colour, and escapism. Alternatively though, more-serious stories can provide deep and powerful beauty. I think of Emma Donoghue's *Room*. The way Ma continues to teach her son how to grow to be a good boy while trapped in a small shed illuminates the power of resilience in the face of adversity. It's exactly the kind of story I want to surround myself with as I struggle to find resiliency after collapsing in the prison of COVID this past year and a half. A parent's love also makes a beautiful and compelling story for me—especially as I try to love Abby through the pain and frustration she's been going through in her own COVID prison. Make no mistake, *Room* is a harrowing story far beyond my own life circumstances, but it has a powerful beauty and a message of hope running underneath it. Presented properly, it should inspire the viewer to see that, even in darkness, there is light. My favourite line from the play is when Ma tells the boy, "Scared is what we're feeling, but brave is what we are doing." I think that message applies to my fellow pilgrims on this path.

It's curious that our production of *Room* has been suspended. The scenery is stored in a warehouse, and the actors are homebound, waiting for theatres around the world to reopen. And I'm here—somewhere between frozen in place and time and knowing, like Ma in the play, that I have to find my way out.

THE SUN DIPS LOWER and lower into the sea. At the precise second it disappears, the fifty people who are now assembled break into applause. The sound shakes me. I haven't heard hands clapping for such a long time. Tonight I have stumbled into a performance on this bluff, and together we have had a shared experience.

And yes, I sure wish I had directed this show.

SHORT WALK / LONG DAY

DAY EIGHTEEN.

Short walk to the town of Villaviciosa.
Only four hours.
Town should be delightful.
Upon arrival: huge disappointment.
Would have preferred to keep walking.
Don't feel like I have travelled enough today.
First time I feel stuck on the Camino.
This town has seen better days.
Quiet.
Dated.
Dull.
Empty.
Picked an *albergue* hoping to meet many pilgrims.
Again, thanks to COVID, people hide in their rooms.
This short walking day feels like the longest day ever.
Longest day.
Ever.
Funny that.

Rumour out in the world: COVID on the rise in the USA.
Spain's numbers are starting to go down.
I've stopped following the numbers of cases in Canada.
I'm not there.
I'm here.
I'm tired of watching numbers.
Very tired of watching numbers.

Tick.

Tick.

Tick.

Too much free time today.
Too much.
I won't be able to get out of this town fast enough tomorrow.

Three glasses of cheap wine on a patio.
They help ease the boredom.
So there's that.

MY FIRST PANDEMIC

WALKING FROM VILLAVICIOSA TO the large seaside city of Gijón today is another long, arduous chore of moving one foot in front of the next. It's difficult to find motivation on the Camino lately. The novelty is wearing thin. Sadly, I'm getting accustomed to the beauty around me so much so that I'm not appreciating it as I should. What I'm conscious of more than anything is how sweaty and smelly my clothes have become. My socks have fumes pouring off them—I'm pretty sure I can see them in the air. It's disgusting. It's all I can think about upon my approach to Gijón. The larger the city, the longer it takes to walk through the industrial sections, then through the suburbs and into the centre of the old town. It's a slow, long-drawn-out entry. Here in Gijón, the churches get swallowed up by a powerful blend of modern and traditional architecture, business, and people.

As I settle into my *albergue*, I commence with my routine of unpacking and spreading Gregory's contents all over my room, including a quick wash of today's sweaty clothes. I reach down into the pack for my collared shirt and, instead, pull out the two letters. I stare at them.

Is it tonight? Yes, it's tonight.

It's been almost three weeks of avoiding them, so I dress quickly and slide one of the letters into my pocket. After racing down the street to beat the rain, which is about to start, I duck into a local bar rather busy with patrons. When a seat opens, I take it and order a glass of wine (which oddly comes with a bag of chips). The rain begins to pour down. It feels safe and warm inside.

I choose the letter I wrote to my siblings twenty-eight years ago. I'm curious to see how I came out to them back then. I open the perfectly folded letter. It begins "Now is the right time to confirm to you that I'm gay. I don't expect there to be overly surprised faces over this one. . . ." *Clever, Dennis— straight to the point.* And then I add: "No more secrets between us. And yes, I know this is against the Catholic faith that we have been brought up with, and in the eyes of the Church, I will not be saved. I struggle with this idea, because I know in my heart that God loves me. But I will not hide anymore from who I am."

I'm captivated with my younger self's honesty. My letter is direct and clear. I'm taken aback, though—shocked—when I read: "I need to confirm something important that you might have been wondering about: Just because I'm homosexual, doesn't mean that I have AIDS."

Breathe.

Right.

My first pandemic.

"All gays will die and go to hell" was said openly when I was in my twenties and the AIDS crisis was growing. My family must have been worried. I keep reading: "We all need a better understanding of what this disease means in the world right now."

It all comes rushing back: a few years after I had started dating, all of the conversations for gay men focused on what the rules or beliefs were around safe sex. Every kiss felt dangerous. Nothing was easy anymore: there were consequences. People died by doing what I was doing. And the twice-annual blood test to check to see if I had contracted the disease was humiliating. First I had to find a doctor who would agree to test me (friends would advise, "This one won't judge"). It was a great pressure to bear the weight of my status of being gay, combined with a serious health concern.

But by far, the worst part of AIDS was watching friends become sick and die. Because of my young age, I had a warning that people older than me hadn't had. I was coming out sexually only after AIDS had taken hold. I think of gentle Murray, a charismatic actor whom I adored, and I remember Scott, the stage manager with a delightful laugh and such a gigantic love for theatre. When I started going to bars at age twenty-three, they were holding on to their lives: both men were dead by age thirty-five. AIDS was cruel. Many lives were lost during this period—and so many of them were artists. I have no doubt we would have a more creative world right now if they hadn't been taken from us before their time.

It shakes me to remember all this. Making sure my family could accept that I was gay was one thing, but hoping they would not worry about me dying was something that I had blocked from my memory. That's a lot for all of us to bear.

I'm living through my second pandemic.

Right.

I survived my first one.

Right.

Twenty-five-year-old Dennis finishes the letter to his siblings with complete sincerity: "I dream that you will be able to share with your friends and family someday that someone you love is gay without feeling apologetic about it. That would make me happiest of all."

And my family did, and they have.

CALLING

"AND WHERE ARE YOU HIKING TO?" asks the woman standing at a washing machine near me, waiting for her load of laundry to be complete.

I've added a rest day here in Gijón in order to tackle the smelly contents of my knapsack. It's early afternoon and the laundromat is empty except for myself and an elderly couple. The woman is looking at Gregory intently.

"I'm walking the Camino de Santiago. It will be over eight hundred kilometres by the time I'm done. And I'm over half-way there."

"Yes, wonderful. I've heard of it. Impressive," the man says quietly.

"Why would you want to walk all that way?" the woman barks.

I watch all of my life possessions spin through the glass window of the dryer. I offer, "Well, it sort of called me."

"What do you mean, called you? Like on your cell phone?" she asks.

I can't tell if she is making fun when she probes me with her questions. She continues, "We're from Glasgow, we spend our summers in Gijón—we have a small apartment overlooking the sea. One of our good friends back home has walked the West Highland Way in Scotland. Do you know it? I think it must be over one hundred kilometres. Sounds bloody dreadful." Her face darkens. "Does this mean you're Catholic?"

"Well, former Catholic."

She nods. It seems like she has heard this before.

The timer on her washing machine goes off. She unloads her wet clothes into a basket.

"I see. But you're walking a Catholic pilgrimage? Because it's calling you?" And with that she walks to the other side of the room to put her wet clothes into the dryer.

"Yes, a former Catholic walking a Catholic pilgrimage," I say to myself.

I try to focus on my spinning laundry.

The woman returns, her clothes successfully spinning in the dryer now. "So, Jews' pilgrimage is to Jerusalem, Muslims' to Mecca. And you walk the Camino. Although you're not Catholic?"

"Something like that."

"It's very good that you are doing this," her quiet husband jumps in. He seems more generally sympathetic and curious. "Are you enjoying it?"

"Yes. I'm loving it—thank you for asking. The nutty thing is everything I own right now is in there," I say, pointing to my clothes dancing in the dryer. "Nothing else. My life now mostly consists of strapping on this knapsack and putting one foot in front of the other."

"And you're following in the footsteps of millions of pilgrims," the man offers. "Good on you."

I open the dryer door. Taking the items out one at a time, it feels as if I have been gifted a new set of clothes. They are finally clean. And ready for the second half of the journey.

"Well, I hope you find whatever you are looking for on this Camino you are doing," the woman says. I have a faint sense that she might just mean it.

WEEK FOUR

PARAMEDIC SAVES THE DAY

I WAKE UP THIS MORNING just before five. There's such a thing as too much sleep. And I'm noticing my morning routine is getting faster as well—I'm a well-oiled machine. I hit the streets of Gijón by an impressive six in the morning. As I head out, it's just me and a large number of cleaners working busily inside stores, getting everything in order. Outside people are washing shop windows, and sidewalk sweepers are pushing away last evening's refuse. It's an early morning secret world of workers restoring the city and preparing it for another day. As I walk, the streetlights go off automatically and quickly plunge the entire city into a semidarkness waiting for the sun to take over. For a precious ten minutes, the shadows come out to play.

Heading directly to the sea once again, I walk on peacefully. The stretch I will walk today—my twenty-third day—from here to the city of Avilés, will be about twenty-five kilometres, an easy day for me now. All the guidebooks report that the route is "rough and industrial" and one of the worst stages of the Camino. I harken back to the dreadful walk into Bilbao, along the noisy highways and manufacturing wasteland. Or when leaving Santander, navigating around the factory spewing chemicals. Could it be worse than that? Not possible.

The first ninety minutes are through a working-class neighbourhood—not unpleasant at all. And there's even a bakery open for a croissant on the run, a new tradition in my morning routine. Up ahead I notice unfamiliar pilgrims. By taking the day off yesterday, I broke the routine of hiking in tandem with the same people. Hopefully this will allow for a slew of new folks to emerge. I promise myself that I will make an extra effort to connect with anyone I encounter. I'm craving companionship once again.

I notice the scenery becoming increasingly grim. All of a sudden I'm walking back in time, to a world of decay and ruin. Enormous exhaust stacks spew ghastly smoke, and gigantic open flames shoot into the sky. All the buildings are covered with the results of decades of this pollution. It reminds me of Dickensian England: dark, dirty, and contaminated. The buildings that remain were certainly distinguished in their day—and there are signs of life in the houses and buildings: dead flowers, broken children's toys, and ratty roosters. Part of this Camino takes me over train tracks, past gas stations, and through tunnels that invite irrational fear. One factory is covered so high in garbage outside that its sign is partially covered. It takes me a couple of minutes to realize that it's actually a recycling factory, and the garbage is on its way to a better second life. It's utterly disturbing. But it does give me something to chat about with the pilgrims whom I eventually catch up with. They are a German couple, and after we laugh together about the view, the man reassures me that his guidebook tells him that it was to be a dirty and dreary day but that things would indeed improve eventually. No matter the language, all the guidebooks agree, it seems. I walk on, as the Germans struggle behind. They're sweet, but not a fit.

A bit of greenery and a few trees appear. And then something happens that I predicted would transpire eventually on this Camino: I'm caught peeing by the roadside. Stopping to have a morning break on an empty country road, looking back and ahead, calculating which bush will be a safe bet, I begin the process. One second later, a car appears out of nowhere, causing me to zip up with embarrassment and continue walking. On my second attempt, twenty seconds later, a pilgrim appears from a forest—he's lost. No bother, I don't stop this time—I finish my pee and chalk it up to the inevitable.

A pilgrim would understand.

And it's just information.

Farther on I come upon a small village comprising about eight humble houses. Under an official sign noting that I have arrived in Los Celleros, I discover a pile of rocks created by passing pilgrims. There must be a couple thousand of these rocks, left by people from all over the world. I stop, take off my pack, and search for the rock. Since this town's name, Los Celleros, is very similar to Bruce's last name, Sellery, I decide it's a clever sign—under the sign—that maybe the rock should be left here. As I zip open my backpack, I realize I'm pulling on an intricately woven piece of neon-green plastic created by my crafty kid. This zipper pull was Abby's gift to my new knapsack. I notice ribbons hanging along a wire directly below the sign. Taking out my handy pocketknife, I cut off a long strand of the plastic. I tie it to the wire—pleased with myself that I have left a memory here representing Abby. Holding the rock in my hand, I pause. It seems too soon to be leaving him here among this epic pile of like-minded rocks. I can't part with it, not yet. I don't feel ready or willing to unburden myself here. I put the rock back in the knapsack and carry on with my walk. Looking back, I see Abby's neon-green plastic string blowing in the wind. I enjoy imagining pilgrims taking in this colourful bit of whimsy, inspired by an eleven-year-old girl from Canada.

The walk in the woods is short lived. As I cross into a traffic circle with Camino signs pointing two opposing ways, a shirtless older man appears on his balcony gesturing animatedly to take the western option. Into a little forest of garbage I go, and when I emerge, I'm looking at the most overwhelmingly gigantic factory complex that I have ever seen. It goes on forever. And I'm now walking alongside a highway with cars barely making room for us pilgrims. In my mind, I decide that any of my usual morning or lunch breaks should be cancelled today. It is dismally clear that moving forward will not include any stopping. Not even an option. I couldn't dare.

I glance back, and I notice a young man approaching—a new pilgrim. Taking the day off has restocked my walking-companion options considerably. The sporty-looking young man catches up to me, and after exchanging the usual test questions—country of origin and the language we speak—we're cleared for further conversation. We marvel at the polluted skyline, and the man repeats what he learned from his guidebook ("It's the worst day. . . ."). Maybe that explains the expression on the face of the kind biker who speeds by and shouts *"buen Camino"* to us in a sort of apologetic way.

My fellow walker is Paulo, from the Czech Republic. He is a trim, tall, and fit twenty-five-year-old man who moves at a fine pace. This is his second time here. His friends don't understand why someone as young as him uses his vacation time for walking the Camino. He doesn't mind the criticism. And he's fast. Paulo is clocking forty kilometres a day. He tells me that after thirty kilometres he finds the real conversations in his head kick in.

Paulo's grateful to talk with someone in English, as most people he's encountered are Spanish speakers and no one is speaking Czech. He has a trait I admire—the ability to engage by asking many questions rapidly of a new person. He keeps the inquiry going. When he learns I'm a theatre director, he grins with enthusiasm. His dad is a professional actor in Prague, and he is a musician, not by trade but by passion. Very quickly he tells me he is genuinely impressed with what I do for a living. It's strangely flattering to have a stranger—especially a twenty-five-year-old one—think I'm cool. Again.

When Paulo explains his current profession, he also explains what he is focusing on with this Camino. He is very straightforward: he's a paramedic and he's not sure if he wants to do it anymore, as the last year with COVID has been relentless. He describes the typical patients he meets in the ambulance: mostly they are young people with breathing problems who are overextended by the stress of it all—and not likely sick with COVID. In contrast, he describes one older man with breathing problems who deteriorated rather quickly in front of his eyes and died. He's wondering at his young age if he really wants to be working the long hours in this way. He seems awfully self-aware. I'm struck by his honesty. "I contracted COVID last fall—and I was stuck in my apartment all alone for three weeks. It was too much. I got very depressed. I couldn't handle it," Paulo shares with me.

We exchange looks.

I nod.

He looks at me and I feel him understand that I relate to his experience: it's not just sympathy.

Paulo sends the conversation back to me and wants to know all about Canada, my theatre, and my child. As I describe my last year with Abby, he nods and smiles with complete understanding. He loves kids. I discover I can be direct and specific around anything, including the theatre, in our conversation. And I've only known him for thirty minutes at this point.

"It's been rough going, not being able to perform live. We've been shut down for a long time," I tell Paulo.

"Did you do any online programming?" he asks.

I shout out, "Yes—and I hate it! HATE it! It's not what we do."

Laughing with me, he adds, "My band went online and I found that performing in small concerts was incredibly painful and unfulfilling."

We talk about how in Spain, with the COVID rules, everyone behaves differently. How absurd it is that people are wearing masks on the beach, carrying surfboards, but taking them off inside restaurants to eat. We connect very easily.

Time passes quickly on our industrial-centred walk, my focus being on Paulo. I haven't noticed the surroundings for a few hours now. As we finish our time together, Paulo puts out his hand to offer a handshake. I'm taken aback. I look down, pause, then take his hand with great confidence. I think it is the third hand I have shaken since COVID began. I savour the moment, grateful. And he wants to see where I work before we part ways. Standing on a busy road on the outskirts of Avilés, we google "Grand Theatre, London, Canada" on my phone, and arresting pictures of the gorgeous theatre pop up. He is thrilled and impressed. It strikes me as funny and just a bit odd that Paulo is the first person I have met after all these days on this Camino with whom I talk about my theatre life. Without missing a beat, he offers, "When I come to Canada, I would like to see your theatre." I look forward to showing him around.

I have arrived at my destination, but Paulo has another fifteen kilometres to walk today. We agree that we will probably not see each other at the pace he's clocking. As I watch him walk away, I like the thought of him telling his dad about me. The world just became a little smaller. He lifted my spirits and helped make a rough day of walking blissful. I hope he sticks with being a paramedic—I have a sense he is exceptionally good with his patients.

CHECKING INTO THE PENSION La Fruta in Avilés, I encounter the most adorable woman in the office. She's nonstop sound and fury—clearly in command and juggling more than a few activities at once. She's shouting orders down the hall, and answering a few different cell phones ringing in her purse, as she describes the town for me. She also checks with me about my hiking plan with such detailed understanding that I have to ask, *"¿Tú caminaste el Camino de Santiago?"*

"Sí!"

And with that she opens a map and shows me the route that she walked ten years ago. We bond over our connection as she shows me the dirtiest room I have ever encountered. It certainly could have been used as a place for sordid rendezvous in days gone by.

Only twelve days of the walk to go.

It will be over too soon.

AN OLD FRIEND

As soon as I start to walk this morning, saying goodbye to the delightful city of Avilés, I notice I have a bit of a swing in my step. This turns out to be a quiet day of reflection, walking through simple pastures, undulating hills, and small villages, with the occasional rooster crossing my path.

Chatting with Paulo yesterday caught me off guard. It was the first time I had talked about my life in the theatre with anyone since I began the Camino, and surprisingly, I reveled in the conversation. It was like remembering an old friend. A kind and generous old friend.

It all comes flooding back: I was tossed into an artistic life thanks to being invited to attend St. Peter's Choir School, a renowned Catholic institution in London, Ontario, when I was eight years old. Vocal music and orchestra rehearsals took place daily. Being surrounded by all this creativity transformed my life. When I was ten years old, I made a declaration for all to hear: "When I grow up, I want to be a theatre director."

At age fourteen, I went to the drama teacher in my very first week of high school. I announced to him, "I'd like to direct *A Christmas Carol*." After a shocked pause, the teacher,

Mr. Patterson, said, "But you're only in grade nine." Regardless, admiring my tenacity, he agreed. (I've since directed *Carol* fourteen more times in my life.) A year later, at the ripe age of fifteen, I was officially promoted to drama club president and expanded the theatrical offerings to a full season of four productions presented at the lunch hour. Admission to these stellar shows was an exorbitant fifty cents per performance. This is where I made real and long-lasting friendships. I met one of the loves of my life, Angela, in the drama club. I see her often now that I am back in London, forty years later.

I completed my master's degree in directing at the University of British Columbia when I was twenty-five years old. A year later I was accepted into the Shaw Festival directing intern program. I had died and gone to theatrical heaven.

In my very first season, I was honoured to assist Christopher Newton, the artistic director, on the comedy *Hobson's Choice*. One afternoon the main actor was not available for rehearsal, so Christopher asked me to help out by "walking the part." Having to act in a play is my nightmare (I'm horrible), and having to do it in front of all these people was my nightmare on overdrive. But of course I jumped up and said yes. We started the scene and I was doing my horrible best with a bunch of great actors alongside me. One actor I was playing a scene with stopped rehearsal, turned to Christopher, and said, "Is this worth it?" with a condescending tone in his voice.

He meant rehearsing with me.

The room went silent. I wanted to run out of there, so incredibly ashamed of what I had caused. But I froze in place. Twenty sets of eyes turned to our director. After a moment, Christopher spoke to the actor directly: "I don't see a problem here."

Huge pause.

"Do you?"

An awkward silence.

Shamed, the actor replied, "No."

"Shall we continue?" offered Christopher.

In that moment, my admiration for this man shot through the roof. I felt respected and protected. That's when I discovered what beautiful leadership is.

I worked as a freelance artist for many years. I'll never forget the first rehearsal of *The Glass Menagerie* at the National Arts Centre when I was the assistant director. In the rehearsal room, only nine people were assembled. To my right was my favourite director, Neil Munro. And on my left was the highly charismatic Kiefer Sutherland playing Tom. I could barely contain my excitement. And when I lived in New York, a planning meeting became memorable for so many surprising reasons. It was at the country home of brilliant illustrator and writer Maurice Sendak (who kindly showed me his original drawings for *Where the Wild Things Are*), and when the meeting finished, playwright Tony Kushner offered to drive me back to Manhattan. Tony drove so fast in his station wagon I kept thinking that the next day's *New York Times* would be reporting "Acclaimed playwright and unknown Canadian die on the interstate."

One of my most joyful and creative experiences was directing John Steinbeck's *Of Mice and Men*. Since the story is set in the Salinas Valley in California, I flew there in advance of rehearsals and walked in the steps of the fictional characters, so that I could experience firsthand what Steinbeck was writing about. These kinds of in-depth research trips would become a necessary and magical way for me to unearth the beauty and joy embedded inside scripts.

When rehearsing the play, I found a note of advice Steinbeck had written to an author. "Your only weapon is your work. Take everything you can but keep your work pure and innocent and fierce," Steinbeck began. "After you have finished it let the sons of bitches have it, but while you are doing it for

God's sake, keep your holy loneliness." I have tried to live by this adage when directing—to follow my own instincts, let the story unfold as I understand it, and then on opening night let people respond to it as they wish. I can't please everyone, nor should I try to. But I must keep my "holy loneliness."

And the work must be:

Pure and

Innocent and

Fierce.

DIRECTING OPPORTUNITIES CONTINUED TO appear, keeping me nicely busy. In my early thirties, Bruce and I lived for a thrilling four years in Manhattan. We fell in love with the city, the access to Broadway, and being in a world surrounded by "our people."

Things were just starting to click for me in New York when I saw the posting for the job of artistic director of Theatre Calgary. Having never run a company before (if you don't include the drama club), I became part of a powerful team—which included producer Lesley ("It's just information") MacMillan and Tom McCabe, executive director extraordinaire—responsible for an annual ten-million-dollar budget. I decided to apply what I had learned running the drama club, and it seemed to work. The support for my ideas by the staff was unwavering. For more than a decade at Theatre Calgary, the team let me explore my impulses, navigate new projects that could have terrified them, and create a culture of great curiosity. The audiences responded, and our attendance grew and grew. Every week was a magical discovery of new possibilities. I was so grateful to be living out my dream while going to "work" every day. My time at Theatre Calgary cemented my lifelong love and passion for theatre.

I have dabbled in the world of opera too. *Carmen* research gave me the excuse to travel to Seville to see the bullfights. I set my production of *The Barber of Seville* on a movie sound-stage—a backstage celebration of the world I love to play in. Watching sixty singers onstage, with fifty people in the orchestra, while sitting among an audience of over two thousand people laughing and applauding my silly, goofy ideas at the Florida Grand Opera in Miami was one of my career highlights.

And then, after eleven years in Calgary, I was feeling the need to move on.

ENTER THE GRAND THEATRE.

Returning to the city where I grew up was not something I had ever envisioned. But when the opportunity presented itself, I jumped at the chance.

"I have an idea."

This is the phrase that I am both praised for and lovingly mocked for at the Grand. When I utter these four magical words, it means a ton of work ensues, thanks to a team who make my constantly flowing ideas a reality.

Together we live by the phrase "World curious and London proud" at the Grand. During these past five years, we have created some magical new productions. We transformed our studio theatre for an immersive version of *Cabaret*—I directed the performers to play instruments while singing and dancing mere feet away from the captive audience. It was so successful it was booked for a five-city, seven-month national tour afterward (COVID ended up killing the tour, indefinitely). We were able to invite the National Theatre (UK) to bring its production of *Barber Shop Chronicles* to us—the only Canadian stop on their North American tour. And of course, being able to coproduce *Room* with our international collaborators remains an incredible highlight.

However, the growing pains have been exactly that—painful. There never seems to be enough money, not enough staff, not enough time, and not enough audiences. Alberta was in the middle of an oil boom when I co-led Theatre Calgary, which made my first go at artistic direction much easier. London is a conservative, midsize city that had somehow convinced itself that its taste in theatre is conservative too. We are changing that, and there's no doubt that everyone has been giving all they have to supporting my vision for the theatre. It's just much harder to produce theatre now—not only at the Grand but truly everywhere. This had already begun to wear on me in the year leading up to COVID.

I've been feeling detached from the "holy loneliness" of creating, imagining, and playing. And I recall today that, for most of my life, it was never like this. A casual conversation with a paramedic from the Czech Republic reminded me that, somewhere along the way, I have lost these impulses. I have stopped being pure, innocent, and fierce. I've forgotten how to play.

RUNNING OUT

WALKING.

One
Two
Three
Four
Five
Six
Seven
Eight
Long hours.
Very long.
Very, very long.
Searching for stores.

NO FOOD TO BE FOUND ANYWHERE.

In my knapsack, I have (left):
Two slices of bread,
One tiny mayonnaise pack,

Half of a mustard pack, and
A few peanuts.
I arrive at a little hotel in the tiny little town of El Pito—
    I've walked through many today.
The *hospitalario* says there will be food at the playa.
Twenty-minute walk farther on, she says.
Make that eight hours and twenty minutes.
Who wants to walk more after arriving at the destination?
Forty minutes later (grump), I hike down a very steep cliff
    and arrive at a beach.
Food for the afternoon finished ninety minutes ago.
The charming bartender sees my sad face and calls out,
    "*¿Bocadillo?*"
Maybe we can make you one, he suggests.
From the back room a resounding *NO* is yelled out.
I burst out laughing, even as I wither in my hunger.
On my way back up to the *albergue*, I pass another beach-
    side restaurant, closed.
I beg the owner to let me buy one croissant. He relents.
With my coins, I look at the candy machine. I choose
    liquorice: I decide that it will trick my brain into think-
    ing that it's new nourishing food, not another bag of
    chips.
I do not want to panic.
I eat one bread slice with mayonnaise and go to bed early.
Hungry.
I walk on at eight in the morning.
It may be another long day in my search for food.
Today I will be a hunter-gatherer.

It's just (grumble, grumble empty stomach) information.

UP AND DOWN AND
UP AND DOWN

THIS DAY HAS ONLY ONE GOAL: finding food. I've saved the one piece of bread in case of an emergency. I must have gone through twenty tiny towns today—one after another—my eyes scouting at every turn. Strangely, no food is on offer. No stores, no bars, no restaurants. I mean, thousands of pilgrims go by annually, and nothing exists on this stretch? Seems like lunacy—or an opportunity waiting to be seized.

The other challenge of today is that, between each town on this stage, I have to go through a forest. And the forest is an escarpment containing a serious depression (insert serious-depression-relevancy joke here). I hike steeply down thirty minutes and sweat my everything off, just to go steeply back up thirty minutes, sweating everything else off. I repeat this eight times. Look for food, go down gully, come up gully, look for food. Repeat. After about four repetitions, this becomes physically painful in my knees and feet. And it's stressful, to say the least.

It's about three in the afternoon and the exhaustion and

hunger have made me light-headed, and I feel like I might start to lose my mind. I come upon a couple of pilgrims and, grateful for a distraction, ask them, *"¿Que tal?"* After an awkward pause, I say in English, "How are you?" Greatly relieved, they answer, "We're doing well." Terry and David are from Dallas, Texas, and are on day four, still getting the hang of things but incredibly upbeat. When I tell them I began my hike at the beginning, in Irún, twenty-four days ago, they are impressed. For a lovely moment, I enjoy being a bit of a Camino celebrity. They want to hear from an expert. It's an appreciated distraction. We walk together for a while and exchange experiences. It certainly makes me feel better thinking I'm not the only one out here. The grumbling in my stomach continues. I'm completely distracted by this, and while I try to carry on a conversation, all I can think of is my hungry state. I'm tempted to ask if they have any food they could share with me. I decide not to inquire, respectful that, as fellow pilgrims, they likely have a limited supply of food.

As I approach the final town for today, Cadavedo, I pray to God to provide me with provisions of any sort. Hiking up an asphalt road, I turn a corner and one small store appears. I pick up my pace and run inside, willing to eat anything. It's fully stocked, but the lights of the store are off, and no one is inside. I hope this isn't a trick being played on me. It's Sunday after all. A woman enters from the back in the dark and proceeds to wait for me to select my purchases. She explains that she is keeping the lights off to conserve energy. Relief. This store is paradise, having more than enough to satisfy, so I run around the aisles a bit delirious and buy as much as I can carry. Anything worth eating, I pick up. By the look on the cashier's face, I'm not the first one this has happened to. I walk down the street, eating terrible dry cookies, and I'm ecstatically happy. I'm going to be ok.

An hour later I arrive at my lodgings for the night. It

is going to be a special treat to stay at the Hotel Torre de Villademoros. The tower was built in the eighteenth century and is still standing in all its handsome glory. The owner and manager, Manuel, explains to me that it was derelict until thirty years ago. He used to play in the abandoned building as a kid. The tower and adjoining house were turned into a small hotel ten years ago and given a new life. My room is a sleek combination of a modern wood-framed bed, with perfect white sheets, sitting inside a stone-walled room overlooking a field of recently harvested hay. Everything about this place is a thoughtful creation.

Later that evening I go downstairs to dine in the artisanal restaurant. It's a striking contrast to the lack of food that dominated my day. All the ingredients used in the restaurant are grown and shopped locally. I walk in to discover a small room with four tables. I sit for dinner, and during my time here, I'm the only person at the eight o'clock seating. Maybe they all signed up for the ten o'clock? Off the handwritten menu, I decide to choose the freshest options possible. Carrot-and-pumpkin soup made with produce from the garden, followed by a tray of fresh asparagus and a lovely bowl of scrambled eggs and spinach. Breakfast for dinner. With a glass of Ribera del Duero Reserva wine. The dessert is a flan covered in warm caramel. After twenty-four hours of being hungry and worrying about a lack of food, I appreciate this meal a thousand times more.

I love Manuel's inspiration and daring to restore a piece of property that has fallen to rubble. And it sits in a very humble village in which the small hotel is the only thing of distinction. Everyone goes about their rustic lives enhanced, but not dominated, by this enterprise in their midst.

While sipping my red wine, my thoughts return to the last year and a half, and I'm starting to wonder if I have handled it a bit better than I had realized. Working through a world crisis is simply that: adapting to the needs at the time. It has not been pretty, and there has been enormous stress related to the fear of possibly closing the theatre and to the emotions of a staff who are understandably fearful, angry, and confused. I'm the co-leader, and I've made lots of mistakes. But no one gave me pandemic emergency training. I did the best I could. And Deb did the best she could. We all did the best we could. And we survived.

Forgiveness enters my heart: forgiving myself, just a little tonight.

I just need to relight my pilot light.

What I hadn't realized, until this moment while enjoying this sumptuous meal in a village somewhere in Spain, is that my response to my troubles was to embark on an act of bold creation unto itself: to walk the Camino del Norte. I've thrown myself into a physical hardship and have challenged myself, to see if I can endure and even possibly flourish. During a pandemic. As if I had created a character in a play and sent the protagonist—in this case myself—on an arduous journey where he discovers he is hardier than he had ever imagined. Is the trial of the Camino a reclaiming of something? It's not like I have been sitting by a pool for a month drinking martinis and pondering my fate. Maybe this pilgrimage is another form of my artistic expression, just realized in a totally fresh way.

From famine to feast, clarity begins to emerge. . . .

CELEBRATING BRUCE'S TRAIL

WAKING UP IN THIS peaceful, serene lodging after a night of deep and relaxing sleep, I look around my room strewn with all sorts of processed food, uneaten. I stare at a bag of nuts, the remaining chocolate cookies, and the highly preserved croissant buns packed in plastic. Yesterday they were my lifeline. I place them back in my bag, hoping I never walk without food again.

Around noon, my usual stopping time for lunch, I sit next to a river under a tree. I have a lovely meal of croissants and nuts, improvised from within Gregory. I'm back on the pilgrim's diet today. As my sore feet dangle in a gently flowing river, I think back to the insights I had at dinner about scripting myself into this gruelling journey. My thoughts wander to a recent time when I had used my creativity for something other than theatre.

LAST SUMMER BRUCE TURNED FIFTY YEARS OLD. We hoped to celebrate this milestone by hiking the Dolomites in Italy, but that trip was cancelled. It was the first summer of shutdown, and there was not much freedom to gather. And besides, I knew what Bruce wanted most: to be with his favourite people in the world. He didn't need a splashy dinner, a surprise party, or an exotic trip, which was fortunate as none of those things were allowed anyway under COVID rules.

I took this birthday challenge to heart and spent weeks secretly planning and scheming. I told Bruce that his gift was a walk with me in the woods for the two of us. That was the setup—and a big lie. What unfolded was much grander than that.

I asked Bruce to reserve a certain day in July. No further details were revealed. I only said he should be dressed for hiking. On the appointed morning, I drove him to the woods just north of the city. At that point he fell for my trap—that the only big reveal was the location: we would walk a portion of the renowned Bruce Trail (which seemed appropriate for a guy named Bruce). The Bruce Trail stretches across nine hundred kilometres in Ontario. While some sections are well trod, this area was not. He looked pleased that we would have a couple of hours together in this way. I handed him my phone and asked him to watch a video of his mother. In the video, Helene was wearing a Bruce Trail T-shirt. With her usual charm, and a bit of a tear in her eye, she wished her son a happy birthday and a wonderful walk. At the end of the video, I presented Bruce with an identical T-shirt. He put it on. I told him to start walking and that I would follow behind. Bruce didn't hesitate or ask questions (he's up for anything), and with an approving grin, he headed off into the forest. He didn't attempt to look back, and he didn't realize that I had disappeared.

About four minutes into his walk, one of our favourite people, Guy, appeared on the trail, wearing an identical Bruce Trail T-shirt. Bruce burst into laughter when he saw his old friend. Guy then invited Bruce to hike with him, and they strolled forward. Bruce wondered where I had gone—but Guy told him not to worry, to be present, and to walk on. Guy supplied Bruce with a bottle of water and a granola bar. An hour later, still on the trail and in the density of the forest, they walked over a rickety bridge to discover Melissa, another of Bruce's favourite humans, also wearing a Bruce Trail T-shirt. "Hi, Bruce, can I walk with you?" she asked. Seeing Melissa, Bruce burst into a big fountain of tears. He realized that this day would be much larger than he had been led to believe. Melissa handed him a mini-bottle of champagne and a cupcake. The two of them walked on, leaving Guy where he was, in the middle of the forest.

This went on all day.

Friends kept appearing and disappearing as if by magic. At midday Bruce walked into a farmer's field to discover his delightful friend Jeanne, known for her culinary talents, sitting at a small picnic table. A lunch feast of her creation filled the table. At the end of the picnic, another friend, Catherine, appeared with two Starbucks coffees. "Walk with me?" she asked. As the day progressed, he walked with his friends Karen, Claire, and then Leah.

At the end of her time with Bruce, Leah handed him an MP3 player and headphones. "The next step of the journey is for you to walk alone," she said. On this audio recording were seven voices from around the world. Friends of his from England, San Francisco, Calgary, and Vancouver had prerecorded themselves walking and talking as if they were physically present. The recording ended with the song "For Good" from the musical *Wicked*—Bruce's favourite song. I was confident he would be a puddle of tears by the time the song ended and he saw his best friend Tammy waiting beside a boulder at the side of the trail. Together they walked the final forty-five minutes. At the end of the long journey that day, they emerged from the forest. And there I was, sitting on a bench, grinning from ear to ear.

Bruce walked for ten hours with his friends, one at a time.

I hadn't seen Bruce all day. Or more appropriately, he hadn't seen me. I spent the entire time shuttling his friends around the route, picking them up, dropping them off, and watching Bruce's progress with the tracker I had secretly put on his phone. He had some theories about how I had put it all together but wasn't quite sure about the backstage logistics.

What I revealed to him after was that I had directed his friends with incredibly detailed instructions. I encouraged them to ask him probing and celebratory questions. They had to bring him a snack and a drink. They were not allowed to give away how any of the logistics worked or comment on what was happening (not, "Isn't it great you are going to walk with all your friends?" or, "Dennis has been working on this for two months," or, "I hope you like this. . . ."). I directed the day, and the concept was specific: two friends going for a walk.

What Bruce didn't see was how I was driving people to the next meeting spot and sneaking them down secondary trails into the forest. Sometimes I had to run quickly with the next guest through muddy paths in order to meet the time-line. I pulled the picnic table out of my car, carried it over my head, plunked it in a field, and then dashed into a bush so he wouldn't see me. I would hide in the trees for the trade-off and then escort the previous friend back to their car. It was joyous for Bruce to have this day with his friends in nature, and it gave me great purpose to create this for him. I loved it, and it reminded me of those puppet shows in the basement I had staged over four decades ago. My self-expression had been taken from me during the pandemic. But Bruce's birthday provided me with an outlet to come up with a big idea and lead a group of people in delivering it. And I have to admit, directing this day for Bruce was a hell of a lot more fun than a few of the plays I've directed.

A week later we had a backyard reunion with these same friends who had walked the trail with Bruce. Our shared experience was a focus of the celebration. At the dinner party, Tammy said to me, "You should make this your next career— building magic moments for others. . . ."

REVISED MOTTO

I'VE BEEN THINKING ABOUT that door sign at that monastery a few weeks back that read, "Welcome, move forward, push."
A new motto springs to mind:

WELCOME
everyone.
MOVE FORWARD
toward beauty.
PUSH
away fear.

SPEED DATING

I AWAKE IN THE EARLY MORNING and look around. Where am I? I know I'm in Spain, but all the hotel rooms have started to blend together. Yesterday reloads in my mind: long walk, arrived in Luarca early last evening from up high, descended hundreds of stairs straight down into the town square.

I remember now.

I know what this means.

What goes down must come up!

As I start walking out of Luarca, on day twenty-four, before the morning sun reveals itself, I have a straight uphill trek: a mad combination of maneuvering maze like roads among darkened streets, while strenuously climbing stairs. In the dark, I head vertically up the streets of Luarca—gaining three hundred feet of altitude in ten exhausting minutes. The view, though, is striking. The streetlights below glimmer and display one of the most uniquely imagined cities, which forms around the natural surroundings—ocean, river, cliffs all meld as one. I stop to take one last look, before I turn and head toward the countryside. The morning is spent wandering farm roads while glimpsing the ocean in the distance. Here the shoreline is less dramatic—the farmland stepping simply toward the sea. No crashing waves or great expanses here. Just the gentle symmetry of land and water.

One female pilgrim speeds by, and later I notice I have caught up to a trio ahead: two women and a man. Watching their walking patterns, I do what I'm sure many pilgrims do—I imagine what their story might be. A straight couple and their friend? Three college kids? At one point, I think it is a mom and her two children. Very hard to tell from a distance.

When I reach the village of Villapedre, there will be a bar open for breakfast. I know this because there have been signs posted for the last two kilometres on our hiking route. One of the things I love about Spain is the lack of large billboards cluttering the view. The lovely exception is on the Camino, where *albergues* or restaurants that wish to encourage pilgrims will post homemade signs on trees a few kilometres before the next town.

I arrive at the Villapedre bar at ten thirty in the morning to participate in a game I call "speed dating—Camino style." It turns out the woman who passed me earlier and the mysterious group of three all stop for a coffee and sandwich. We exchange our standard greetings, ask where each other are from, and the speed dating begins. Whether intentional or not, it must be a universal activity with all Camino hikers— shopping for potential walking dates and using coffee stops as a speed-dating opportunity. We are all sitting outside on the café patio, and I begin talking with the one who was walking quickly. I can tell she isn't actually looking for a date—she's in a hurry. A shame really, because she's a delight and a fireball of energy: she's from Poland, and I like her smart, direct intensity. She speaks with great clarity and informs us she is on a forty-kilometre-a-day plan. Before I can ask her name, she blurts out, "I have to go!" Mere moments later, she's gone. There's so much about her I would like to know.

Turning to the mysterious three, I learn they are all Spaniards. The man is from Barcelona, and the women are from Zaragoza, a city between Madrid and Barcelona. The three of them only started walking together this morning. I guessed wrong. Knowing that they speak the same language and are already partnered together makes the speed-dating game tricky. It may be too difficult to break into this newly formed party.

One of the women is bubbly and totally my type. When I press her with a couple of questions, her smile remains, but her understanding of English is not as strong as I first sensed. Oh, how I wished my Spanish words were better. At one point I ask her if she is enjoying her walk. To that, she issues a little chuckle, a sure sign that she doesn't understand. I love to offer *si* when I don't know what's going on; I have received a similar strange expression in return many times—my feeble answer in no way answering the question just asked. The man and I talk about Barcelona, one of my most favourite cities in the world. The problem is—and I sense it—that he has just connected with these two women, and though he might like to walk with me, he already has a sure bet. And who knows—maybe his future wife.

I put on Gregory as the others put on their knapsacks, but then I make the rash decision to hurry it up and move along. This speed date was a bust all around. I won't see them again. As I leave, they barely notice me. I walk on alone, and I think, *Well, at least I tried.* And I saved myself from an awkward second date. . . .

SAFE?

ALONE AGAIN, I CALCULATE that for roughly 75 percent of my time out here on this particular Camino, I have been walking solo. In addition, since this year's Camino has been much more sparse than other years, I'm spending hours on this path in isolation with little to no interaction with other humans. I find going through forests alone a bit unnerving—something about wild animals and thieves in hiding waiting to pounce on me. Unexpected sounds make me jump. I'm more alert when I don't have space around me. And I am always a bit more relieved when I'm walking in open expanses.

THERE'S A REASON THAT I sometimes walk in fear.

Ten years ago, a few years into my tenure at Theatre Calgary, Bruce, Abby, and I were interviewed for an article for the city paper, the *Calgary Herald*. It was a sweet honour—two dads and a two-year-old baby. The photographer came to the house, and the writer spent a significant amount of time with us writing the story. It became a feature article in the Life section of the paper, with a large colour photo of us. We are seen in our home sitting together on our couch with our delightful child between us. A happy family. When talking with the reporter, we held nothing back, proudly sharing stories of our family and how it was formed through adoption. A group of social workers banded together to create a nonprofit to serve the needs of women faced with an unplanned pregnancy. And same-sex couples were welcome to apply. Through the open option, the birth parents choose whom the parents will be. The child doesn't need to wonder about their past, because there can be contact. Abby's birth mom chose us, and when Abby was two months old, we brought her home. We shared all the details of our story with the *Calgary Herald* easily and openly. It was a positive experience for us, as we wanted to promote the vital world of adoption. We also wanted to celebrate the incredible women who work at Adoption Options, the agency who matched us, for making it possible for us to form a family.

A few days after the story ran in the paper, I received a letter at the theatre.

It didn't have a return address—that should have been my first clue. I opened it to discover a small piece of paper with a few words scribbled on it: "sodomite" and "give that baby back" and "leave our country." No complete sentences—just threats. I was shaken. I didn't know what to do with it. I was shocked, angry, embarrassed, confused. I told no one except Bruce. Walking home that night alone, nervous with fear that I was being followed, I walked briskly, looking behind me every couple of minutes. As I approached my condo building, I scanned the horizon to double-check for anyone following me. I raced inside and locked my door—after checking every room of my home for evidence of intruders.

Two weeks later I received another letter with the same handwriting. This time I opened it carefully, assuming there might be a need to lift fingerprints off the contents. From the envelope, I pulled out a picture of me that was taken from a theatre publication.

There was a big "X" across my face in red ink.

I called the board chair of the theatre, Maggie, and shared with her what was happening. She was quick to take action and called the Calgary police. The next day I met with Officer Wright of the Calgary Police Service. A police file was opened on my case. He offered his perspective on how these kinds of people work and explained to me that I needed to be vigilant and alert at all times. I was clearly distraught, and so, near the end of the conversation, he stopped and looked directly at me. He knew I was a public figure in the city, and his words were perfectly directed. Officer Wright said, "You strike me as a smart guy, so I think you can use this incident for good. You can rise to the challenge and not let this take you down. Do something with this."

Later that day I started telling people.

I shared the news with my closest colleagues at the theatre. They agreed we had to be vigilant and that everyone needed to know, for my safety, in case this person decided to drop in at the theatre. As the days went on, my fear turned to anger. It became exhausting and tiresome to be constantly watching my back every time I went into a public place. I was angry that this anonymous thug had control over me. That I was being stalked. And of course, it filled me with regret that I had exposed my family to danger by being so public.

There was no third letter, but the damage was done. A stranger had managed to instill the fear in me that I was somehow lesser than others. Ultimately, I do understand that these are the actions of unstable people and that their wrath is directed more at my type than at me specifically. And as I have carried on, I have been a bit more cautious with to whom I tell what. But we remain a family that does not shy away from our story in public places.

Even so, every now and then, in a dark corner, or a shady forest, I do wonder if that person from ten years ago is still following me—with darker intentions. It's not logical, but it still haunts me. I walk the Camino fully aware of my surroundings at all times—what is behind me and what may be to come. It's a practice I've had to learn in the last ten years.

BIG RIPE TOMATO

ONCE A WEEK, I treat myself to an accommodation that is a bit more expensive, unique, and comfortable than a typical *albergue*. A few times I have been lucky enough to stay at restored historical places with the "agritourism" label attached to them. Usually this means an old house beautifully renovated on the outskirts of a town. In La Caridad, I'm delighted when I arrive at Hotel Rural Casa Xusto. The lobby's warm, stone and wood-beam interior is lovingly crafted, and with only ten rooms, it feels like a private home.

Rodrigo, the host, is soft-spoken as he checks me in. I ask about the bar that I can see just off the lobby (an excellent option in a tiny hotel), and he responds with a hesitant offer of what time it might be open. I instantly feel the power and the pain of these pandemic times. People are just not gathering in the same way, making running a boutique bar challenging and costly. I don't push him for specifics; I understand. We carry on with the check-in, and then Rodrigo asks, *"¿Cerveza?"* As I'm quick to light up, he disappears from the lobby, returning with a cold Galician beer and a clean glass. I'm loaded down with my backpack and poles, so he walks me to my room, setting my drink on the bedside table.

After a delightful afternoon rest in my plush attic space, I wander into the small town in search of dinner. I am early—as always—and the locals haven't emerged post-siesta yet. As I watch the shop owners open their stores for the evening, sweeping the entrances and arranging their goods on the sidewalk in hopes of enticing people passing by, a forceful feeling overcomes me: a deep sense of gratitude.

The local people along these routes have a lot to navigate—pilgrims walking by their homes, filling their streets, constantly getting lost. Everyone who lives here is automatically made a host, whether they like it or not. What would it be like to have strangers from around the world pass by my house in Canada on a daily, or hourly, basis? Would I be called to support them? And maybe because it is a pandemic year, the sense I have is that these people speak from their heart when they say *"buen Camino."* The dramatic decrease in pilgrims has changed their landscape, and their livelihood. *"Buen Camino"* this year feels like a battle charge: it will be a good Camino, dammit! I adore hearing the phrase from the cyclists the most—they speed by wearing their bike outfits, going rather fast. They yell it out with a crazy sense of glee. But every time it is said, no matter who says it, I'm jolted with a sense of appreciation and humility. *"Buen Camino"* is an understatement.

I find a grocery store and pick out bread, cheese, and meat for my lunch on the road tomorrow. Through trial and error, I have come to learn it's always best to pick solid items that will withstand the jostling/shaking movement of Gregory on my back. As I arrive at the bakery section, I see Rodrigo—my kind hotel host. Through our masks we say hello, and he introduces me to his wife. He isn't dressed as formally as he was earlier in the day; it's delightful to see him now in jeans and a T-shirt.

The next morning, when I'm at the front desk checking out

with a clerk, Rodrigo appears in the lobby chatting with a few patrons who are coming down for breakfast. Looking out at the rain that is coming down, we agree it's not the best way to start a long day of hiking. We laugh and we shrug. I'll take what comes my way. Rodrigo is called into the breakfast room. With my tab settled (the *cerveza* turned out to be complimentary), I put on my raincoat, lift Gregory onto my shoulders, and add a rain slicker tarp on top of it all. It's many layers to manage now, but at least it will keep me dry for the first few hours. Rodrigo is nowhere in sight when I wish to say goodbye, so I head out onto the rainy street, regretting that I was not able to give my thanks personally. As I turn the corner of this well-preserved building, I see Rodrigo standing in the doorway at the back, keeping out of the rain. He is holding a bright-red tomato in his hand.

"I went to the kitchen to get you this, *señor*. My neighbour grows the best vegetables in the village, and I thought you could enjoy this today," Rodrigo says. He presents the tomato, and then places it gently into a plastic bag.

"Rodrigo, that's very kind."

"I didn't see you buy anything fresh for your lunch last night. You need fresh, always," he tells me. "It won't be a pleasant walk today, but at least you'll have this. Maria next door knows how to grow tomatoes."

Speechless at his kindness, I take the tomato in the bag, thank him, and begin my walk. He stands in the doorway, watching me head off. I must be a sight: a walking garbage bag with an extended arm holding a tomato.

I will not damage or drop this gift.

I walk forward in the rain.

Stretching into my fourth week, I have been on this journey for an incredibly long time. At the start of this trek, back in mid-August, the weather was hot and the beaches were packed. Today, as I walk through towns and pass three alluring beaches, a striking contrast is present: the rain and the cold have emptied the places out, and now that we have rolled into September, the crowds are noticeably smaller. At one empty beach-bar stand, I notice only one patron. On a second look, I realize that it is actually the bartender sitting down with nothing to do. Is it time for me to go home? Not yet.

It's now a challenge to gain entry to most churches unless it's close to a mass service. Midday I see one church standing triumphant on a cliff near the ocean. It would be an excellent break from the pouring rain; I could receive a stamp (and possibly even pray?). As I approach, I see a pilgrim attempt to pull open the door. It's locked shut—this one with a padlock.

I've done my best to keep the tomato intact, switching it from hand to hand throughout today's walk. The hardest part of my day is near the end. I cross the expansive and incredibly high (vertiginous, unnerving) Puente de los Santos bridge in the pouring rain. The winds batter my tarp, making it a loud and messy walk. I cling to the railings, seriously hoping not to be swept over and down to the raging river far below. When my feet arrive at the other side of the bridge, it also signifies that I have crossed into the last section on my journey.

I have walked into the province of Galicia, home to the city of Santiago. I feel an urgency to my time here: it's running short.

Too short.

I'm not ready to be done with this Camino.

I arrive at my quaint seaside hotel in Ribadeo overlooking the boats in the marina. Fishermen are bringing in their catches of the day, seafood is being sold at the docks. The smell of ocean and fish is pungently strong. Inside my room, I complete my arrival routine: warm up with a fresh shower, drape all wet clothes and coats on every surface in the room. Now dry and restored, I sit in the middle of the bed, lay out a towel, and proceed to prepare my dinner. I know that I'm mere steps away from excellent seafood restaurants offering local delicacies. But as I begin to slice and assemble my sandwich, I know there is nowhere else I would rather be tonight than with my big ripe tomato.

THE OTHER LETTER

In the dark of the morning, I say my goodbye to Ribadeo, to the smell of fish and salty ocean air, and I give my thanks to the Atlantic Ocean: it has provided so much pleasure, but now it's time to head inland toward a church in a city two hundred and fifty kilometres away. I notice the province of Galicia honours the Camino significantly by a much higher quality of way markings on this portion. They are more consistent and better built. The signs even have the countdown in kilometres to the city of Santiago on each post. Clearly this Camino is an important business for Galicia.

Entering this province feels like beginning the final chapter. The end is in sight. It makes me feel a bit anxious today, wondering if I have accomplished all I have set out to do on this journey. With that in mind, the other unopened envelope in my bag is calling to me. I need to look at it before the trip ends. It must be resolved.

The letter is from my high school teacher's wife.

We were supposed to call our teacher Mr. Patterson, but very quickly he allowed some of us to call him Jim. He was a gregarious, charming, big-hearted soul. He loved teaching and he loved the theatre. He encouraged me constantly, and we created a bond early on. Jim taught me how to stage a scene with actors, how to keep the energy moving, and how to keep the focus on the key speakers at all times. Through my high school years, he was my hero. I would call him more than a mentor; he was a father figure. My father at home didn't understand or encourage my passion for theatre. But Jim did.

Jim was married with five kids. I became another child in the Patterson family. His wife, Anne, was always welcoming when we had meetings at his house. When he mounted the school shows, he gave all the hours in the day to work on it. It was a joy to be around him—he shared his passion for theatre with anyone who would stand close enough to soak it all in.

He hosted the best opening nights in the world and was loved by his students.

I went off to university and we stayed in touch—he always wanted to hear about what I was learning. For my graduation, he bought me a drafting table. When I made my professional directing debut at the Shaw Festival, Jim and Anne made a special effort to be there on opening night. I was thirty years old, and I still hadn't told Jim officially that I was gay. I was certain he knew, but still, until it was said out loud, it wasn't necessarily true. So when I was visiting Jim and Anne at their hotel just before opening night, I let it slip out simply: "Oh, by the way, I have a boyfriend named Gavin." That's all I said. Jim received the news politely and we moved on. I was relieved to do it: to come out, one more time.

Three weeks later a piece of mail arrived in my mailbox. It wasn't from Jim. Surprisingly, it was from Anne. As a devout Catholic, she thought it was her duty to inform me that living a homosexual life was a sin. I remember sentiments such as "going to hell" and the classic "you can be gay, just don't act on it, and repent it for the rest of your life." I think there must have been Bible quotes.

I picked up the phone and called Jim immediately. I asked him if he knew about the letter. He said yes and began to cry on the other end of the phone. He repeated the phrase "I never should have let her . . ." over and over. I wasn't angry—I was hurt and confused. By the end of the call, Jim had apologized for his part in this. I told him I would deal with Anne separately. He promised he would do right by me.

A week later I wrote Anne a letter in response but also sent back to her the original handwritten letter she had written to me. I thought this was a punishing way to send a message: keep your opinions to yourself. The truth is I photocopied her letter, and also my response, so that I would have evidence to refer to if needed. Almost twenty-five years later, I am walking the Camino with copies of those letters in my knapsack.

I can pinpoint the time I officially became a "former Catholic" to the moment that I opened that letter. I decided back then that, with all due respect, the Catholic Church was a club in which I was not welcome. I have decided to reread her letter here on one of the most Catholic pilgrimages there is. I'm hoping maybe one event clarifies the other.

As I walk this holy path, these conflicting thoughts move with me. The letter burns in my knapsack. I have been considering the options once I reread Anne's letter. Will I burn it? Leave it in a church here? Send it to her with an updated response? At one point last week, I thought I should not read it and should just throw it in a random trash bin.

But I have decided that I will read it soon.

I don't want to leave it until too late, and I don't want it to colour my experience arriving in Santiago. Is that possible? Being unaffected? After all these years?

• • •

SIX YEARS AFTER I RECEIVED THAT LETTER, an important thing happened in Canada: same-sex marriage was legalized in the province of Ontario. In front of us, Bruce and I discovered a choice that we never imagined we would have in our lifetime. We now had to choose to NOT get married. Funny that.

While we were still living in Manhattan, Bruce and I came back to Canada to visit our family for a week in the winter of 2004. We dashed up to Perchance, our cottage, to check on it. It's not winterized, so we had the wood stove working at full force to warm the place. While waiting for the cottage to heat up, we went for a walk along the edge of the frozen lake. We hiked for thirty minutes in the bracing cold. Finding a perfect place in the sun, we sat on the frozen lake for a break. We unpacked our hot Earl Grey tea, cheddar cheese, and crackers. I took the cutting knife, and into the ice in front of me, I carved the following question:

"Will you marry me?"

Looking down, Bruce read the words but didn't believe them. "For real?" he asked out loud.

Taking my knife again, I carved "4 real."

We sat together on our frozen lake, looking at each other.

I held my breath.

He said yes.

Back at the cottage, we called our parents. They were thrilled.

We decided that the best place in the world for us to hold our wedding would be, of all places, the Grand Theatre. Long before I ever imagined I would be the artistic director there, I rented my future place of employment as a wedding venue. We booked the theatre for that spring, on June 19.

One hundred and fifty guests were invited to join us. Many of them flew up from New York. The ceremony took place on the landing of the upper balcony, with a full view of the renowned proscenium arch behind us. Our mothers walked us in. Instead of a "best man," we both had "best friends" stand for us: Shira for me, and Tammy for Bruce. When it was time to sign the register to make it official, the officiant, Lee, surprised us by saying to the guests, "This is the point of the wedding where you all typically chat to each other while we sign a lot of papers. I want to remind you all that, in this country, this wedding represents progress. As Bruce and Dennis sign their wedding papers, history is being made. I invite you to pay attention." While a gathering of our favourite people watched closely, a quartet playing in one theatre box, the five of us signed legal marriage paperwork in another.

At the reception, I asked my mom what her favourite part of the ceremony was. "In your entire life, I've never seen you kiss anyone," Mom stated. "It fills my heart to see that you are loved."

Our friend Jennifer, who had flown up from New York, said, "I've never been to a gay wedding." To which I had to admit, "Neither have I!"

There was one person missing that day. My high school teacher Mr. Patterson.

Four months before the big day, I sent Jim an email asking him to participate in the ceremony. I thought it would be deeply moving to hear him speak, and to be a powerful presence as a father figure on my big day. Since we had resolved the issue with his wife years ago, I assumed he was committed to our friendship. A few days later his response was short and simple: "I don't believe in gay marriage and I won't be attending." I never found out how much of this response was his and how much was his wife. I imagined she drew the line and he caved. We never spoke or saw each other ever again. A few years later he died, unexpectedly.

I miss Jim—and feel a deep sadness that he didn't get to see his fifteen-year-old drama club president become an artistic director. He would have loved that.

I'll open the letter soon.

SPANISH KINDNESS

I PASS MANY MUNICIPAL *albergues* that are empty and have remained so since COVID began. I imagine the pilgrims at the picnic tables, on their bunk beds, at a communal table. I can almost see the dust that two summers of lying fallow have created. I have to admit to myself that I'm getting terribly lonely—and that it would be a healthy thing to talk to other humans soon. It's been five days mostly hiking alone.

As I walk the roads over rolling hills and through lush farmlands surrounding Ribadeo, I notice up ahead those three mysterious Spaniards from a couple days ago. It looks like their date has been successful, as they're still together. I'm happy for them, and not wanting to engage, I try to slow down and hold back. When they look in my direction, there is no cheering for that nice Canadian guy they met at speed dating. They seem to look right past me. As I come closer, I decide to do my best to say hello, but also simply intend to move past them as fast as I'm able. My instigation of *hola* gets little reaction. I ask them how their day is going and receive a decidedly lukewarm response. What is this energy? I try one more question but, feeling truly in the way, begin to walk ahead, defeated that even simple questions are awkwardly answered. My instincts were correct on that speed date. It all feels embarrassing—they didn't pick me the first time, and I am being rejected for a second time. As I fumble ahead, I hear some rumblings from behind. "Where are you headed to today?" seems to float into the air and is sent my way. It must be them speaking and it must be to me, I decide. Curious. Why are they trying now? I spin around and with a big smile offer, "My goal today is Lourenzá." They nod in agreement, for they are going there too.

All of a sudden, like they had a secret signal between themselves, the three of them start walking faster and join my pace. I'm being swarmed. They begin asking me more questions. I'm being courted by three people at once. We are now unexpectedly walking together.

Has our second date begun?

It's hilarious how awkward this phase is. I'm not sure if the attempt is actually a mistake: *Keep going*, I tell myself. It's like learning to skate—terribly painful to begin but great fun once you learn. The bubbly one does most of the talking to me with her excellent efforts at English. I notice that the other woman doesn't look at me, but that the man smiles with a calm, gentle warmth. It's a bit overwhelming to be talking to three people all at once now, so it's a relief when two of them walk ahead and I'm left with the bubbly one. She tells me her name is Marina: "My name is like the sea—where the ships come into harbour." Lovely. We connect easily, and I feel guilty that I thought she didn't understand English as much as she does. She is solid—not perfect—with her language. And she reveals to me that the other woman, Elana, is currently learning English and is incredibly shy about it. Very quickly I realize that I'm a bit of a threat to her. Elana would smile at me but then would look away. I suddenly feel it is my task to solve that connection.

After a while, a rest stop is suggested. It's decision time: keep walking or take a break with them. We all stop. We make small talk, eat our apples and granola bars, and drink our water. I watch the three of them connect intimately. I look for signals: do they want me to go? It doesn't seem so. We walk on together. Upon further conversation on the path, I discover that Marina has been a trouper on this hike: she broke her leg skiing two years ago. Her leg is doing fine, but now her knee is acting up. Resilient, she wouldn't be stopped. I've been walking for three hours with her with no complaints or sign of the pain that she must be in.

At thirty years of age, Marina has a master's degree in architecture. She tells me that, since she was ten years old, she's always known what she wanted to do—design buildings. The focus of Marina's Camino is to sort through her work/life balance. Recently she left her job at a prestigious international architecture firm. She was managing many projects for them, including new buildings in Saudi Arabia. After a year in this role, she was highly stressed and found herself far from the core of the work she likes to do—designing. When she speaks about this, a true melancholy comes over Marina. I congratulate her for asking the big questions before she commits fully to her career.

As the day moves on, I find time with José, a fifty-year-old man with two grown children. I've guessed his story wrong from afar: not as old as I thought, and not looking for a girlfriend. We talk about the shared milestone of turning fifty years old. His celebrations were cancelled, thanks to COVID. When I ask him what he does for a living, he explains simply that he works in an office. He has no desire to explain further. José's been at the same job for fourteen years but is feeling a strong urge to move on. I'm starting to think the Camino should be rebranded as "a career crisis–counselling hike." With the exception of Joy, most people I've met here are really struggling with finding their work/life balance. And currently too much work and not enough life means no balance for everyone.

We walk together for six hours, and by the time we arrive at the hostel—we are staying at the same place, as fate would have it—a friendship has formed. I cannot believe the turn-around from what had begun as rocky speed dating a few days ago. Wanting to have dinner with them this evening, but not wanting to push my luck any further, I go for a walk into town and don't check in with them regarding their evening plans, fearful of rejection. It will work out as it is meant to.

IT IS AN IMPORTANT DAY BACK IN CANADA: it's morning there on the first day of grade seven in a new school for Abby. I decide to break my plan to not use videoconferencing, as I am desperate to see what Abby looks like today. First days are important and make me very nervous. Going to kindergarten when I was a child, I was overwhelmingly shy and wouldn't let my mom leave me on the first day. There might have been some crying. I still remember it. My mom had to take me home. This happened on the second day too. On the third day, after a bit of time had passed, I told my mom, "You can go home now." I suspect I had made a friend in the class? It's a legendary story in our family: the kid who cried taking his first steps in education goes on to obtain his master's degree in the arts. Go figure. Based on that history, it's important to me that my kid has a great first day. However, truth be told, for Abby it has never been such a big deal—in terms of nerves. She likes school and being around large groups of kids.

Over the last two weeks, since camp ended abruptly, something beautiful has been happening back home. Bruce and Abby have found their groove. Bruce sends me encouraging notes about the joy the two of them are having. It seems to me that, in addition to being parent and child, they are becoming friends. And today on the video, she looks like a bright, incredibly happy preteen. What more could I ask for? She is in a chatty, optimistic mood and relieves me of any guilt for being so far away. I beam with pride across the tiny phone screen.

After the call, I continue on to the town square, and I discover the San Salvador Monastery. Looking up close, I see the attention to detail in the stonework is incredibly meticulous. And here I'm able to obtain a stamp for my pilgrim credentials. While I soak in the majestic scale of it all, Marina and Elana emerge from the front doors of the cathedral and, seeing me, suggest an "early" dinner at eight at the hostel. I play it calm and cool and accept their invite, casually (while wanting to blurt out, "OK—you like me! You really like me!" to quote Sally Field).

Arriving promptly at dinner, I'm surprised to see everyone already seated—waiting for me.

One spot is empty.

Mine.

No food or drink ordered. All warm and inviting eyes turn to me.

I also notice a new pilgrim at the table. His name is Dick, and he is someone the group had walked with a few days before. Dick is from Belgium—well spoken and energetic. I peg him to be in his midsixties, but eventually he reveals he is an impressive seventy-four years old. He's a retired traffic officer: he was in charge of investigating gruesome traffic accidents in order to make the roads safer. Dick adds more colour and kindness to the already bountiful feast.

This newly formed band are now sharing a pilgrim's meal: *pistou*, fish, homemade wine, and laughter. It feels like we are in the kitchen with our grandmother, who even sits with us and dines. The hostess, who is also the cook, has the most incredible warmth about her. Local liquor shots are shared. Marina translates and provides context for the English speakers—a

kind gesture of inclusion. I sit beside Elana, and we start "courting," exchanging words back and forth. Elana is a party girl, so she loves to shout out English phrases like "Let's do it." I encourage her as much as I can—and word by word, she shares her English. It's much better than she thinks.

Maybe it's the wine, but at one point the conversations are so loud, and occurring in at least three languages, that I have an out-of-body experience where I'm watching myself from above—surrounded by this international energy of kinship. It goes very quiet in my head as I tune out the noise, and tune in to the power of community. I'm surrounded by very good people of the world.

There are three kinds of dessert brought to our table, and we attack them gleefully, forks and spoons reaching over each other's plates, bites being taken. COVID be damned, the six of us share openly.

We all push through our own insecurities today and emerge as friends.

GROUP OF SIX

SITTING AT THIS TABLE, I'm reminded of a special gathering I host annually at Perchance, our cottage. I lead an artist retreat I have named fondly "the Group of Six."

When the cottage was relatively new to us, I was sitting on the dock with my good friend Louise. I was reading a *Vanity Fair* article about Beatrice Monti della Corte, who turned her fifteenth-century stone barn in Tuscany into a miniature writer's colony and invited writers from around the world to hide away and write. The article explained how it was her great joy to host these writers and the only ask was that they join her for dinner. Imagine those dinner conversations while spaghetti carbonara, warm focaccia, and a good Chianti were passed around. I was drawn in and intrigued. I suggested to Louise, an innovative producer and big thinker, that it would be a lovely thing for Bill Whitehead to transform their house in France in honour of Tiff. Louise's face lit up: "Why don't you do this here? Create an environment for artists to be together. You have this stunning place. Make it a retreat. And make sure there's wine!"

We named it in honour of the famous Canadian painters of the area in the 1920s, known as the Group of Seven, but cheekily adapted it to the ideal number of places set at a dinner table: thus, the Group of Six was born.

That summer Louise and I cohosted the first three-day retreat. We invited four other artists and crafted a program to fill the days. In our group were a director, a producer, a designer, a visual artist, and two actors. The structured time would be at meals: guided conversations over dinner with wine. For the rest of the day, everyone was free to canoe, swim, hike, and rest. The themes were intentional. Night number one: celebrating the artistic life. Night number two: sharing the pain and struggles of an artistic life. And the final-day brunch: living a brighter artistic life. Over the years (I've hosted it nine times so far, skipping a few summers in a fifteen-year span), we have had hysterical laughter, incredibly vulnerable sharing, heartbreaking tears, gigantic hugs, and always skinny-dipping en masse. Every time, I partner with one person to ensure that a great mix of people are invited—no one is allowed to know more than two people in the group, including myself.

I suspect I created the Group of Six out of a personal need to surround myself with like-minded humans. I love the combination of being both the host of the event and a participant. And for me, I get to be myself—one of the six, playing along. I get a great charge out of seeing people's lives transformed, but I'm also left with encouraging thoughts and inspirations from these new voices. The magic of the Group of Six is the willingness of the people to jump in. I love observing the fear in their eyes when we begin the first exercise, where I can see them thinking, *Oh my God, what have I signed up for? I don't know these people.* And then, mere minutes later, people share their most intimate and vulnerable selves with strangers. It's powerful stuff. Artists are constantly giving of themselves, and this retreat replenishes their artistic souls. I know for me, guiding is such an honour and a self-expression. It parallels the Camino in striking ways.

The last time I hosted the group, ten months ago—the COVID edition—it included one of the most incredible humans I know, Jan, and one of my newest friends, Emma Donoghue. Emma admitted to me afterward that her kids were amazed that, being such a private person, she would willingly hang out and discuss intimacies with strangers. I loved getting to spend time with Emma in this way. There was also a ridiculously inspiring music director and two talented actors I desperately wanted to know better. We opened our hearts and laughed and laughed and laughed.

I guess Group of Six is a way to keep my pilot light lit every year, as needed. I didn't think about it at the time, but that's what it was.

I have a dream to reunite all the artists who have ever participated for one last Group of Six, once I have completed ten of these retreats. On the final night, we will sit together at one epically long table by the lake. That year, the final year I will ever host, it will be a celebration of the Group of Sixty.

I thought of hosting another edition of the Group of Six this past summer, but unlike last fall, I couldn't muster the energy to envision it—or, mostly, to take responsibility for it. It didn't seem like something I could bear.

As I look up at José walking around the table filling everyone's wine glasses, Marina describes excitedly the house she has begun to design for a friend. I decide that, without any planning, tonight is this year's honorary Group of Six—the International Edition.

WEEK FIVE

EASY PEASY

A TEXT FROM ABBY BACK IN CANADA wakes me up this morning, saying upon returning home on the first day of grade seven, "I've made new friends Daddy!!!" The best words a parent could read. She goes on: "And please call me Asher from now on. My pronouns are now they/them. I'm nonbinary." My child has been trying on this new identity for a few months, switching back and forth, but has decided that the start of this school year signals a new beginning for her—I mean, a new beginning for "them." Of course Bruce and I support anything they wish—it will just take time to adjust to a new name. But I like it: Asher. We applaud Asher's clarity and confidence to be more open and responsive to more possibilities in their life. Bruce reports that Asher brought a couple of new classmates home for dinner, and they stayed for hours. School life in person resumes. Parental sigh of relief.

José had told me that he wanted to start walking early this morning, at seven. I wasn't exactly asked—it was just assumed I'm part of the group now. Pulling myself awake and appearing at the appointed time, I'm ready with Gregory on my back, headlamp strapped on, standing outside under a streetlamp.

We quietly head out of town and into a dark forest, our essential lamps leading the way. We spend forty-five minutes in the darkness. It's eerie, and romantic at the same time. Guided by my own light, and the bounce of the others', I have to step carefully as we walk up a roughly carved path through a farmer's field.

The experience walking with others is completely different than going alone. As a solo trekker, there is a true sense of freedom ambling forward with no pressure to keep a tempo. Stopping or pausing at any moment is easy to do. With a group of five, the dynamics are more complex. First, I'm always aware of where I am in the pack: seldom in the front, usually in the middle, and trailing at the back when feeling the need of a breather from the others. There is an expectation for the group to stay together—not too far of a distance between the first person and the last. But there is also a very strong code of respect that allows people to walk at their own pace. We did not sign up to walk the route as a team, so the generosity and freedom are pretty astounding to experience at the same time. Someone pauses to rest, the group responds. Walking with people makes the time go by faster, no doubt. The friends are my focus, so the landscape drops away.

Elana is speaking mostly in English as we walk together. We decide to play with language lessons—learning each other's mother tongue a bit more. I'm taught some words in Spanish related to directions: "left" (*izquierdo*) and "right" (*derecho*) are easy enough. And nothing is sweeter than three people helping out. The phrase for going forward or straight is *"todo derecho,"* which is pronounced "to-dad-a-red-e-o." I keep mispronouncing it "toda-e-recto." This produces much laughter. Elana offers in perfect English, "If you are saying it like that, you are saying my man thing is standing up." We all howl with laughter.

I introduce a catchy little phrase, "easy peasy," when we talk about the mountain we have to climb up and over today. It's a simple slang phrase that is actually more difficult to translate. Elana is confused. I explain the rhyme and the meaninglessness of it. Comprehending, Elana teaches me the Spanish equivalent of "it's not hard," which is *"fácil."* Up the six-hundred-metre mountain and down the other side, the words "easy peasy" and *"fácil"* can be heard, shouted out intermixedly.

After three hours of walking, we stop for coffee, and Marina asks the owner of the lovely café for the typical dessert of the region. We all have a decadent cake, named after the town we are in, Mondoñedo. Made of almonds and local crushed berries, it's delicious.

I ask these pilgrims what Spaniards think of the Camino.

"My friends have all walked the Camino. We talked about it in school," Marina offers.

"Si! There is much respect," Elana adds.

"But surely some people don't like it?" I ask.

"Only the ones who hate how busy the paths become with pilgrims," says José.

Marina jumps in: "It is a rite of passage among people I know. It is part of our religion, and therefore we value it. It is an honour to be here."

At lunch in Abadín, with Marina's maneuvering, we end up in a crowded back room with thirty locals. Together we are all enjoying a full three-course meal with homemade wine for ten euros. The wine is so undistinguished at these places that they always place a bottle of mineral water beside the bottle of wine. That's to dilute the taste of the wine—the bubbles are a lovely distraction—masking the lack of flavour cleverly. I notice the corks of wine bottles previously opened are collecting in a corner basket in the restaurant. I start a game of cork tossing.

We cause some commotion in the room, and ultimately José is the winner—scoring the only hole in one. Everyone cheers for him.

This is the end of our time together for now. I have a hotel booked in this town, and they all need to walk farther. My overplanning restricts any sense of spontaneity. I do wonder if I should just forfeit the place here and keep walking with them. However, I'm relieved to hear that Elana and Marina will be arriving in Santiago next week on the same day that I will be, and we plan to reunite at the end of the Camino. I'll see them again, so I will pause here as planned. Let's hope our reunion happens.

This will be the last time I see José, however. He has to pick up the pace in order to catch a train back to Barcelona early next week. Near the end of lunch, he says to me, "Dennis, I realize we will have to say goodbye soon"; a really warm expression crosses his face. "It has been a pleasure to meet you. I have enjoyed your positive spirit."

I was thinking the same thing.

"José, you are a great guy. I've loved our time together and meeting you. Good luck with work." This quiet soul contributed much to the group with his generous smile and calm demeanour. I never discovered what "I work in an office" meant. It never mattered. Truthfully, I was a bit sad that he wouldn't, in fact, be marrying one of these two women. I felt close to José, even through our imperfect attempts to communicate, and yet we had spent a total of two days together. But that was plenty to sense the character of this lovely man.

On the stairs outside, the Spaniards stretch their arms wide open and offer me warm, strong hugs. And off they walk together as I first met them, chatting animatedly as they fade into the distance.

Easy peasy.

THE HONOUR OF A
SCALLOP SHELL

WALKING SOLO AFTER TIME with new friends is always a funny sensation. In some ways, it's like a new start. I wake up very early, have coffee in bed (first time on this trip), and enjoy the freedom of setting my own pace. It's a shorter walk today, only eighteen kilometres—five hours of walking from this small village of Abadín to the larger city of Vilalba. The journey will take me through country roads and fields. As I head out the door, a little later than usual, I'm rewarded with thick fog that has overtaken the town. It's already nine in the morning, but I can't see very far down the street. I know there are expansive views I will be missing, so I take this all in stride. At one point it is so foggy that visibility is reduced to about thirty feet. Being bathed in this natural occurrence is joyous, providing me with a unique perspective. I feel safe and held and marvel at the majesty of this morning.

I pass two men who must be in their seventies walking softly along the Camino. I witness the one man asking the other to walk ahead so he can take a picture of his silhouette.

It's lovely. As I come up to them, I compliment them on their photo idea. They look like high school sweethearts in the bodies of old men. It's adorable. We share a knowing smile.

It's a quiet day on the walk, filled with many flowing streams and lush greenery everywhere—yet again, I'm provided with new landscapes. Every day remains a discovery of surroundings on the Camino del Norte. After a coffee break, I return to walking across farmers' fields, and I come across a small bridge over a stream. I notice a man sitting on the bridge carving something out of a wood branch. And he has on display about fifty small wood sculptures and pieces of jewelry. In my twenty-eight days of walking so far, I haven't encountered anyone selling anything along the Camino path. I become flustered, and we exchange modest greetings as I pass. I walk on and immediately regret not stopping. Why not buy something from this artist for my child? If my kid was here, they would have looked carefully at his treasures, complimented his work, and then begged me to buy something. I stop and consider going back, but by then it feels awkward and too late.

It dawns on me in that moment that kindness and compassion cost us nothing. The brave one is the artist who has brought his crafts to the bridge, daring to sit there and be present. All I had to do was receive him. I could have chatted, I could have complimented, I could have bought something. But I literally decided I was too busy. I was too busy? Doing what? Walking? What was I so afraid of? Talking to strangers?

As I stand still feeling stupid about my actions—or non-actions—it dawns on me that maybe the Camino is working. I think about my friend Lesley and "It's just information." And this time the information is stop and engage next time. Becoming more insular at this point is not the right direction—the Camino is inviting me to shift how I respond to the world. It is even presenting lovely artists directly on my path to engage with. Could it be a sign? Of course it could be—if I choose to see it that way.

I walk on.

I find myself on a narrow country road that is fenced in with shards of large patio-stone shapes—something I haven't seen before. It makes the path specified and keeps me focused on a course. All of a sudden, I hear a tractor coming my way ahead of me. I proceed forward, thinking I will be able to squeeze by. As the tractor approaches, I realize that the farmer is driving while leading a herd of very large cattle down this road. There must be twenty of them. I squish myself against the side of the path and hope for the best. A procession of impressively sized cows passes my way—some of them less than six inches from me. After a few minutes of meeting the slow-moving cows, I hear barking and two dogs appear at the rear, working hard in their efforts to keep the cattle moving. They do their job with precision and focus—and barely even acknowledge me. Just another day at work for these dogs, deep in concentration on their task.

I turn a corner in the woods and come across a humble little house with an ancient wood-beamed shed. Inside the opened shed is a harvest table with items for sale: tomatoes, cucumbers, fresh cheese of the region, walking sticks, and the classic Camino pilgrim scalloped shell. Camino commerce twice in one day? I look in awe at this lively assortment.

This time I stop.

I enjoy the whimsy and makeshift arrangement of it all, and I pick out a few things: a wedge of *tierno* soft cheese and an iconic Camino scallop shell. It's set up as an honour system, so I take my time, pay properly, and snap a few pictures. I'm about to move on as a woman appears from the second-floor window of the house, thanking me effusively and wishing me *"buen Camino."* I don't run this time—I thank her and compliment her on her cheese, which I've unwrapped and already taken a bite of.

The appearance of this second stand feels like a gift when I see there are scallop shells for sale. The scallop shell is a powerful sign of the Camino: it's used as another way to mark the trail, besides the arrow, and pilgrims are known to display one shell on their knapsack, to clarify that they are on the journey. I've been waiting to buy one when it appeared to me in a special way.

Now, when anyone asks me where my shell came from, I can describe to them a little country lane, a kind woman who assists pilgrims, and the improvised market stand in her shed. . . .

IT'S TIME

WALKING INTO A MIDSIZE CITY is a bit of a jolt to the system after many days in the country. Vilalba seems to be a highly efficient, blue-collar sort of place. In the town square stands the Iglesia Parroquial de Santa Maria. In comparison to the highly ornamented and soaring churches that I have encountered so far in Spain, this one is rather humble. It doesn't dominate the street or its surroundings.

I pull at the church door, and surprisingly, it opens. I enter and look around.

There's a life-size sculpture of Jesus lying in a tomb at the back of the church, blood-stained hands at his chest. Awkwardly encased in glass, this sculpture is kept separate from parishioners so they can't touch it. Directly beside this is a shelf holding fifty prayer candles. But here, presumably to prevent fires, it's electronic. The system for lighting a candle is comparable to a video game. Fifty cents lights one electric candle, one euro gets you two electric candles—those are the options. If you put a coin in the slot, a candle will light up. It's about as tacky as you can get. I can't imagine dropping in a coin and taking it seriously.

I walk down the aisle, passing the empty pews.

A young boy of nine or ten with curly black hair comes out of the vestry in his white robes, going about his duties preparing for mass, which is to begin in an hour. He brings in the altar wine and the chalice and lays out vestments with great precision. He arranges the objects, adjusts their placement by an inch or so, and ensures everything is set just right.

Sitting in this empty church, I feel compelled to confront my past here and now. I know the letter written by Anne, my high school teacher's wife, is in my bag. I can feel its presence, having been brought along for these many days. It's time.

Reaching into my pack, I find the letter and open it carefully. I count six pages, written in a distinctive cursive style. The letter begins: "I want to admit that I'm a sinner. And because of that I strive to live according to the will of God." Her self-criticism is a jarring way to begin. On page two she addresses the reason for writing directly by informing me that "the church clearly tells us that homosexual acts are acts of grave depravity, and tradition has always declared that those acts are intrinsically disordered. . . ." The coldness and assuredness in which she writes about something she has no insight into astound me. Disordered? And how does she know this? At the bottom of page four, she instructs me that "homosexual persons are called to chastity. By prayer they can and should gradually and resolutely approach Christian perfection." Anne is suggesting that my only way to survive this life and not go to hell would be to live a lonely, unloved existence. Not the most compelling suggestion. She finishes by saying, "Dennis, I'm offering you support to live in freedom—freedom to be good." This proposal doesn't seem like it includes room for a great deal of negotiation.

I finish reading her lengthy letter.

I pause.

I ponder.

At the time I first received the letter, I was devastated, embarrassed, guilt ridden, angry, and confused. I was thirty years old, had worked through considerable shame and guilt for my sexuality, and this attack by a supposed friend was the final straw. Anne's letter produced the absolute opposite goal to what she was striving for: I left the Church because of her cruelty.

And now I sit in silence here in this pew trying to understand the emotions running through me, waiting for some feeling to take over. But I have an unexpected reaction—pity. I pity Anne for feeling that she had the right to set the moral compass for another human. That she would attack a person who meant so much to her husband. It caused me great pain, but I can't imagine what Jim had to endure because of this. I pity her righteousness.

I unfold the copy of the handwritten letter I wrote to her in response, dated September 1997—twenty-four years ago. One sentence stands out: "I will accept your apology for your cruel letter when we meet in heaven. God will forgive you for your lack of knowledge and judgment of others. . . . Please do not pray for me. Pray for tolerance and greater knowledge in the world."

I'm struck by my boldness.

I didn't apologize or justify.

I stood up for myself.

Watching this altar boy work so carefully to prepare for mass, I wonder if he walks with the faith of God in his heart. It's been a long time since I let myself feel anything close to faith. Once I severed my relationship with the Catholic Church, I stopped believing and praying. I hope that boy's faith is strong. I am leaving all feelings about this letter (negative and otherwise) here in this church today. And I won't contact Anne—no need to now.

I'm going to keep the letter though.

That's not an option I ever imagined before beginning the Camino. I wanted to destroy the memory and all proof of it. But this is part of my story, and it is not something to be ashamed of or something that I need to make disappear, I am realizing. When Asher sorts through my things when I pass away (no time soon, I hope), I want them to look at these words and be aware of my history. They might be just a tiny bit proud of their dad's letter of response. And I hope Asher has it easier: that Asher looks back at their life and can speak to the supports that moved them through, not the obstacles that attempted to slow them down.

I place the letter safely back in my pack, feeling at peace with it now. I kneel and make the sign of the cross before I walk back up the aisle and head outside into the bright light of the day.

YO SOY DE CANADA

RESTLESS WITH THOUGHTS AND POSSIBILITIES, I wake up early this morning in Vilalba. I'm trying to put together the connections between what I discovered yesterday. It's never occurred to me before that any time I received a negative reaction to being gay was a direct result of being open or public about it. I started the conversation; I picked the fight. In all cases I should have expected it, prepared for it, and managed it. Why was I so surprised every time that someone might have a negative reaction to my honesty? Here is what it comes down to for me today: I need to remember that it is a privilege and honour to have this voice. I have to carry on and stop claiming "victim" when attacked. There are so many others without this privilege of voice. And the more our voices are together, the more we can impact change.

Lofty thoughts. And it's only seven in the morning. With these energizing ideas in mind, I head off for the day.

Now that it's September, the mornings are starting off with a real chill. Travis, our guide on the West Coast Trail earlier in the summer, often said, "Be bold, start cold" as a way to think about dressing on the morning of a hike. The idea is that within an hour your body is likely to warm up and you'll be stopping to put a fleece back into your knapsack. This adage has been very helpful so far on the journey—to dress for the day ahead, not the moment in the early hours.

This morning I keep my body moving. It's cold. Heading out through fog again, I also know that today I'll pass the marker for the final one hundred kilometres, which is considered the "minimal" amount of walking if you want to be able to officially claim your status as a pilgrim. Many people only walk the last one hundred kilometres. In order to test a person's fortitude, a pilgrim has to receive two stamps a day from this point on. It is quite regimented. An accommodation can be one stamp, but the other should be more religious in nature. That's been tricky this year, thanks to all the COVID closures, but still the rules are the rules. I've been collecting my stamps but am finding it a bit of a distraction—or maybe a competition in which I don't want to play. I'm challenged by the idea that I have to prove I walked this far. Isn't my word enough? I will keep collecting stamps for now but hope I don't fail at this task.

The number of pilgrims increases significantly on this final stretch, since this is where we get the "vacation" pilgrims (sorry, I said it). I know that in two days, when the Camino del Norte merges with the Camino Francés, I will see the numbers increase almost instantly. Joy has described the effect as an on-ramp joining an epic busy highway of humanity. I'm not all that thrilled to imagine the days ahead. On an online forum yesterday, a woman wrote, "I just merged from the Norte to the Francés, and if one more person says '*buen Camino*' today, I'm going to hit someone." I laughed. Another person on the forum didn't find it so funny and responded to the woman with "you should have stayed home." I laughed louder.

I'm a bit surprised to see that the pilgrim attendance increases already this morning. I'm used to a few hours alone every day. Not today. There is a pod of pilgrims surrounding me that I'm unable to shake, and ten of us walk together for about four hours, mostly spaced out, but still awkwardly in view of each other. The feeling among the pilgrims is decidedly different. There doesn't seem to be much interest in new friendships being formed, just the focus on getting to the finishing line.

At the town of Pobra, there is a choice—a quicker route for five kilometres along the highway or a slightly longer route of seven kilometres. I'm usually one for the shortcut, but I decide to take the more scenic route, which promises a lunch stop at a park by a stream.

Arriving at the park just on the outskirts of town, I discover a beautifully curated oasis: stone tables and benches, a little waterfall, and trees dripping with greenery. As usual, I arrive early for the typical lunch hour and the park is empty. I've packed some cheese and meat and decide to relax and enjoy my time here. However, at precisely one in the afternoon, three families arrive in six cars, with copious amounts of picnic provisions in hand. It seems that lunch is always the major meal of the day—in or out of a restaurant.

It's lovely to see the ritual of a picnic unfolding. On this sunny Sunday afternoon in glorious Spain, all is right with the world. As I'm packing to go, a woman in her forties asks me if I will take a picture of her extended family. Delighted, I also use this as an opportunity to practice my Spanish—asking the woman to tell me who is the *abuela* (grandma), which ones are her *hermanos, hermanas, primos* (brothers, sisters, cousins).

One of the sisters asks, *"¿De dónde eres tú?"*

I respond quickly, *"Yo soy de Canada."*

EVERY TIME I'M ASKED where I'm from on the Camino, I love to reveal the news: I'm Canadian. I haven't always been the proudest Canuck. Growing up, I felt we were always in the shadow of England and the United States and everything we did was in the pursuit of being as good as them. Canada is still represented by the monarchy, and an overwhelming amount of our culture is centred around being one of the colonies. We import the great plays from Shakespeare and Shaw. Telling our own stories was rarely considered. When I was in school, we studied European history, not the history of our land. And in the theatre, Broadway is considered the pinnacle of success. Even though I grew up without the internet, I knew every show on Broadway and all the gossip I could find.

We didn't talk about Canadian plays. We talked about everyone else's culture, not ours.

I was about to begin a dress rehearsal for a play I was directing at the Stratford Festival twenty years ago when Bruce called. "Sit down," he said. "Do you want to move to New York?" He was asked to take over as New York bureau chief for BNN News, broadcasting out of Times Square. Even though I was directing at the largest theatre in Canada, we thought we had won the jackpot. We were moving to New York! We were moving to THAT city. It was an incredible four years in Manhattan, and we soaked up everything "the greatest city in the world" had to offer.

Since being back in Canada, over the last fifteen years, things have slowly started to change. Canadians are becoming celebrated for the traits that we were formerly mocked for—being good, kind people. The world is starting to awaken to the power of "nice." I don't mind that moniker, and I do think it is apt. I am nice. However, since the political upheavals in the last two years, alongside our niceness Canada is also confronting its own atrocities. The recent discovery of secret unmarked graves of indigenous people at residential schools over many decades is justifiably stripping away our "nice" moniker. Bit by bit our colonial ways are being reexamined. This path to a better Canada has been part of a radical awakening. We have decades of work ahead of us to right our wrongs and to make ourselves truly the good, kind people we have been characterized as. However, now we are beginning to tell our own stories—kind, good, ugly, and true. Being witness to this stage of Canada's growth is both upending and uplifting. At one time I thought I would be happy living out my life in another country, but now I know Canada is my home.

I TAKE A PRETTY RESPECTABLE PHOTO of the family who have gathered for their picnic, but I think if it is going to be memorable, they need to find some originality and silliness in this shot. I provoke the six little kids to show me their goofy faces. They jump around and giggle. I call out:

"Say 'Canada'!"

And a glorious gaggle of Spaniards scream: "Caaaaaanaddaaaaaa!"

It's a great shot.

ANGEL

WHEN I ARRIVE AT BAAMONDE, there are two distinct options for heading toward the town of Sobrado. The traditional way is thirty kilometres. And the direct option, with no places to stop—except one *albergue*—is ten kilometres shorter. Feeling totally guilt-free since it's an official option, I set off on the shorter route.

I'm in my last week on the Camino, and as I enjoy a snack of a fresh apple and granola bar on the stairs of yet another locked church, I have a strangely specific thought: I'd like to meet one more person on this Camino with whom I can connect on a significant level. My head is full, and I'd like to download my ruminations with a like-minded pilgrim. It's a bit of a specific request, but nonetheless I make it to the universe.

I'm hoping that sitting on church steps might help. I walk on.

Parga Natura Alojamiento is a new accommodation created by the lovely couple Vincente and Isobel. Realizing the way to help make the shorter route popular and possible, they renovated an abandoned building into a six-room *albergue*. The arrival to their place is daunting, walking through a series of abandoned, crumbling buildings in order to come across a new, expertly renovated oasis. It's a sparkling little place with a ridiculously low cost for one night's rest. And dinner is optional; however, given that there's no place to walk to within a few hours, it's easy to sign up for a meal. When I step into this restored building, the attention to detail is evident. Local paintings are perfectly hung in the communal room with large windows overlooking the fields surrounding the property. Isobel shows me where to put my boots and where to hang my poles. She shares with me the details of the house as if it were the first time she's ever explained it. Her freshness and intimacy of connection make me feel at home. In the kitchen behind her, I can see her husband preparing *paella* in an impressively large skillet.

As I'm about to take Gregory up to my room, the Polish woman from speed dating walks in. I'm delighted. I haven't seen her in a week. At the pace she's been walking, I'm impressed that somehow I'm keeping up. It helps that she took a rest day to explore the beaches of Ribadeo. But still, we are here together. It's a chance to discover more about her.

After one of the best naps on the journey, I return to the common space and settle into a *cerveza* as three cyclists arrive, equally exhausted and as exhilarated as I was to discover this place. I find the Polish woman outside; I still don't know her name, nor she mine. We begin the classic Camino update of our journeys. As we speak, I notice one of the cyclists appears outside. He's listening intently and joins the conversation, with perfect English, to congratulate us on the long journey we have been on. A Spaniard, he is on a "long overdue" visit to the Camino. He's spending five intense days on his bike, and while he's loving it, he's convinced the time he has allotted isn't long enough. He envies the time I've spent.

He asks me where I'm from.

"Yo soy de Canada."

"Oh, I love Canada. I've been there many times," says the man. "Do you know London, Ontario?" he asks.

My jaw drops to the floor as I explain that I do indeed.

It turns out that, when he was a teenager, he spent a summer in London on an exchange program to learn English. I explain that I work at the Grand Theatre. He is curious and asks lots of questions. After I'm able to jump in with questions for him, he reveals that he, too, works in the nonprofit arts. He is the founder of a music school in South Africa.

Our connection is instantaneous, and my attraction to this person's intelligence, wit, story, and curiosity is intense. I can't believe my luck—I literally put my request to the universe a few hours ago to meet someone extraordinary and here he is. Valentino is forty years old, was born in San Sebastián (my lover), raised in Bilbao (thanks Frank Gehry), and schooled in Valencia (ooh, add this to my must-go list). He now splits his time between the sexy party island of Ibiza (cool) and Cape Town, South Africa (super cool).

Valentino drills me with questions about my work, my theatre, and my family. His questions take me to places that I haven't gone in other conversations. I'm inadvertently ignoring the Polish woman. She politely excuses herself and goes inside. Valentino and I carry on talking our "art talk." We converse in big, beautiful ideas: he explains that the vision of his school, Bridges for Music, has three principles:

Curiosity.

Empathy.

Creativity.

We are literally speaking a shared language together—the language of artists.

The conversation is electric.

In his twenties, Valentino was a powerful force in the club scene of Ibiza, a party capital where hip young people spend the days on the beach and nights in the clubs dancing till the sun comes up. As he describes it, he programmed bands and singers for the infamous disco Amnesia (known as "a place to forget your concerns of the day"), one of the largest clubs in the world; it hosts six thousand people a night. We share the enthusiasm of programming events and watching people discover new artists. When he turned thirty, he tells me, his life started to become routine, and his creative excitement was dwindling. It didn't feed his soul anymore. He went on a sabbatical (sound familiar?) and travelled the world.

Valentino found himself in the slums of Cape Town. There among the shantytowns, he heard electronic music that he describes as outrageously original and alive. Kids were making music by wiring together any electronic parts they could find. It was mind blowing for him. And that is where the seed was planted. Quitting his lucrative job, he focused on creating and establishing a school for electronic music for young people in Cape Town. Now, ten years later, Bridges for Music is fully operational, and supported by major musical artists in the industry. He speaks about all of this with incredible humility. I'm starstruck—not by the musical artists he knows—but by his vision and commitment to young people.

Our conversation returns to me and why I'm on the Camino. I can't explain the power he has over me, but I don't hesitate—I tell him all the gritty details. A couple of times I pause awkwardly, and like a gentle therapist, he asks softly,

"What are you not saying?"

And then I say it.

And many times he finishes my sentence with complete and perfect understanding, nodding in gleeful agreement. He understands what I have been going through, as he's experienced many of the same challenges. Through this stranger, I'm feeling heard and validated. He understands my stories, empathizes with my experiences, and commiserates with the challenges of making art during a pandemic.

Time flies by quickly, and suddenly it's dinnertime. There are ten of us sitting at seven tables. Our host brings out a large skillet filled with freshly crafted seafood *paella*. Our small group breaks into applause as Vincente divides it up among us all. I don't taste it much, though, because my focus is on my dinner mate. I am unable to see anyone but Valentino.

I fall for him, in a completely platonic way. But I do fall. Deeply engaged, not sexual, intense. The two of us carry on, talking about my family, his girlfriend, and life choices. As I tell him the story of how we formed our family when Asher came home, his eyes light up with joy. "That story would never unfold in Europe as it did in Canada," he offers. Almost everything one of us says is instantly understood by the other.

Dinner ends, the other guests disappear, and we continue talking over wine. Vincente clears the tables all around us. He asks us to turn off the lights when we're finished. Eventually we realize everyone has gone to bed. We will be closing the place at ten in the evening—for pilgrims, incredibly late.

Our last shared idea of the night as we are turning out the lights: Valentino suggests he should bring a concert to the Grand Theatre, and I volunteer that I would like to come to South Africa and work with his students.

We go to our rooms—but I don't sleep. I can't sleep.

I lie in bed overwhelmed by thoughts.

My head is spinning.

And then I feel this odd sensation from within:

My pilot light.

I can feel a flicker.

Just a flicker.

Then a small blue flame.

It has been relit.

I'm not certain at first, but then I feel a warmth come over me.

Yes.

My pilot light has returned.

I've heard it said that there are angels on the Camino. People who offer extraordinary or super-simple moments of assistance or guidance. I've brushed off this idea as exaggerated folklore. Until now.

I think I've met my angel.

And the message this angel delivers is clear: "I see you. You're an artist. Don't give up. What's next?"

Valentino arrived in my life on the Camino at the exact moment I needed him to. Three days before completing my walk into Santiago, in one precious evening with him, I articulate, discuss, and debate the thoughts that have accumulated over these past five weeks. He was a beautiful listener who instantly understood and appreciated all that I'm struggling with.

It seems too good to be true.

In the morning I'm happy to see him come down to breakfast. We speak for a few more minutes, and he shares with me the power of meditation, something he does daily and has done for fifteen years. It helps explain his calm, focused demeanour. And it feels like a useful step for me moving forward. We take pictures together, we hug, we exchange our contact information.

"It's been a pleasure to meet you," I offer simply.

"I couldn't agree more. I look forward to hearing from you," Valentino replies, accompanied by his gorgeous and inviting smile. I could have easily spent the week with him, but he has to bike his one hundred kilometres to Santiago today and complete his Camino. And I have to get moving. I have a long day ahead, with a rekindled life.

Angels come in all types. I've met my Camino angel: a Spanish cyclist named Valentino.

MONASTERY IN A STORM

I THINK ABOUT VALENTINO most of the morning, replaying our conversations over and over as I hike along in the pouring rain. I didn't sleep much last night, feeling the thrilling challenge to turn his important inspiration into action. My brain has kicked into overdrive. The way Valentino fearlessly switched directions—but retained his passion for music while pivoting—seems like an exciting challenge and offer.

I imagine/create/dream/strategize a possible new direction for myself:

Go solo: form my own nontheatrical theatrical company.

I have always loved curating moments for people: travel planning, creating dinner parties, hosting artist retreats. I have always wanted to direct a parade, plan a wedding, stage an awesome concert in someone's backyard, produce an opening ceremony, or even plan someone else's hiking trip. And I like to think that these adventures would bring people closer to themselves. These experiences would be one of a kind, off the beaten path, undiscovered or unexpected adventures. As I walk in the dense morning rain around me, I toss around some ideas, until suddenly I land on a possible name for my new company:

"Hidden Beach: Beautiful adventures, directed."

Enjoying this idea, covered thoroughly in a sturdy blue plastic tarp given to me by Elana last week, I walk on in the downpour elated, navigating a busy asphalt road. At one point a car slows down, and a young man rolls down his window and calls out to offer me a ride. Without missing a beat, but with a great big wet smile, I yell back, *"No, muchas gracias."* And I start to laugh. Who turns down a ride in the pouring rain? A pilgrim does. He joins me in laughter and drives away. I'm sure he's thinking to himself, *Silly, wet pilgrim. . . .*

Beautiful adventures, directed.

WALKING INTO THE TOWN of Sobrado dos Monxes, I have the sense there's a powerful force here. At the heart of the village is a five-hundred-year-old monastery, which will be my home for the night.

This monastery is one of the largest in all of Spain. It's impressive from a distance and intimidating up close. My sense is that, over the centuries, religious people who were moving from village to village would need rooms for a temporary stay. The tradition continues. They advertise this as a place to "clear your mind" and "be present with God." I couldn't turn down this possibility: one night in a monastery, with dinner and breakfast included.

Feeling bolstered by my flickering pilot light and the possibility of a newly formed company (not so much because I would start this new company right away but because I am deliriously and delightfully dreaming again), I enter the monastery just before five in the afternoon. Well, I enter the only open door, which is the gift shop. It's high end and stylishly laid out. I'm a little taken aback that wine and beer are available for sale. I can't imagine that in a gift shop at a church in Canada. It seems off brand to me. The shop volunteer calls the *hospitalario* and he appears. As he is giving me a private tour of the grounds, I feel like royalty being guided around these hallowed halls. The monastery is shaped by a series of interior courtyards—all connected. Everything is a considerable distance from everything else. As the man shows me the dining room, I explain to him that I will be leaving at six the next morning. I have the longest walk of my journey tomorrow—forty kilometres. The breakfast is always at eight in the morning at the monastery, but I explain to him that I understand and don't mind missing breakfast. He is distraught. I reassure him.

As we walk to my room, we pass the hostel section that would usually host a hundred people every night. It's been closed through the pandemic, and as I walk by the empty shoe racks (where pilgrims would deposit their stinky hiking boots outside), I think about all the people who would not experience this fine place. I'm given a key for my simple room, but it's clear that I'm going to be locked in the monastery for the night. My host leaves me.

That's when an epic, roaring thunderstorm begins. The biggest downpour I have experienced in my travels so far consumes the sky. The rain is pounding the roof, lightning periodically illuminates the empty courtyard below my window. It is thrilling. I'm incredibly grateful to be inside and dry. And worry for the pilgrims who are caught in this mess. I'm safe, though, inside a monastery. Have I caused the thunderstorm? Is God unhappy that I have dropped in for the night? I can't help but wonder if maybe he feels that there is an intruder here. This is a serious consideration.

I shave my stubbly face, zip on the legs of my hiking pants, and attempt to look as respectful as I can. I've been invited to attend a religious service—forty-five minutes of prayers called vespers. I want to be presentable.

It continues to rain.

At the appointed time, fifteen minutes before seven in the evening, I wait in the courtyard. A monk appears, and I follow behind him. We walk up a set of dark, expansive stone stairs. He moves aside a temporary barricade so that we can go through. It feels incredibly secretive and surreal. Lights are turned on for me in darkened hallways. The monk makes a joke in Spanish, and when I explain my lack of comprehension, he switches to English and with a posh British accent says, "No problem, all languages are covered here. Welcome." He escorts me into a room where chairs are set in a circle. The monks will be in the middle, and the guests will be on the outside. I sit in a socially distanced wood chair. There are very few lights on—I can't see across the room. As other people arrive, I begin to wonder: *Will this service be in the dark? What have I gotten myself into?*

The thunder continues to rumble outside, and occasional flashes light up the walls.

At exactly seven in the evening, I hear the bells chime in the monastery clock tower. At the same moment, lights are turned on and monks float in. They are wearing white robes, with full hoods and very long sleeves making their arms invisible. And they're not wearing medical masks, like we are. There are only ten monks and ten guests. For some reason, I had pictured a few hundred people in a church setting with pews. It's an intimate gathering—not at all what I had imagined.

This time together begins with a series of prayers intermixed with song. At the organ is the monk who brought me in. Throughout the service, lights go on and off—a well-orchestrated and staged event. And to be honest, the semi-darkness is relaxing and inviting.

The rain continues to pour down.

I'm watching these devoted men, for they are all men, pray together. One of the older monks stands beside a young monk.

He is clearly giving him guidance. There's a lot of head nodding and pointing to each other. It's lovely and powerful to see the old passing instruction on to the young—the traditions continue.

I know it's not a church and I'm not at an official service, but I do use the time to think and, dare I say, to pray. In this semi-lit space, the gentle singing is very peaceful, and deeply inspiring and conducive to thought. I'm feeling at home. This familiarity makes me realize (admit? concede?) that a huge part of my story is growing up Catholic, taking part in church regularly, and attending a Catholic school until I was eighteen years old. This religion has had a hand in shaping me, giving me structure, and encouraging important principles such as "Do unto others as you would have them do unto you." I loved my school days singing in choir. I had a beautiful childhood in this respect. Rather than discounting my past as a "former Catholic," maybe I should instead say "I grew up with the Catholic teachings." While I disagree with some of the Church's doctrine, and there is no doubt it damaged my sense of self in my adolescent years, I did find my way forward.

For the very first time in my entire adult life, I am grateful for the Catholic Church, and the good it has done for me.

The monks are now singing in unison. The voices aren't what you'd expect to hear at the Vatican, and the volume is low. That's what makes their efforts all the more honest. I feel their passion for their beliefs.

The lights switch off again: there is only one little light now, illuminating the younger monk as he begins to read from the Bible.

I feel my mom's presence. She is sitting beside me, in this darkness. In her final years of life, when I would visit her, we would go to mass together. She would always be grateful when I would agree to attend with her. I would escort her to a pew, her movement made difficult by three decades of living with the disease lupus. We'd sit together, and mom would go very quiet. She was with God.

In this monastery, here in the dark, I say a little prayer of thanks. Not for my mom this time, but for the Catholic Church. There was one extraordinary gift that religion gave to my mother: faith. Her deep, unwavering faith in God, the powerful doctrine of the Church, and the belief in a meaningful afterlife were always central to my mother's life.

Her faith was her pilot light.

Yogi always said that her children were her proudest achievements. I think she would say her devotion would be second. She endured a great deal through the years with us kids and her husband. And she always insisted that we go to mass, and that we abide by the rules governing the Church. We had mixed results with this request (think Church of Burger King), but we all knew, and did not question ever, that Mom had an unshakable faith in God. And that faith served her well.

As she grew older, Yogi liked to spend time chatting with the priests after mass. They would be rather chummy. She would share with them everything about her life: they became part of our family. As an adult, one time when I came to visit the small village where my mom lived, she wanted me to meet the priest after mass. I shook his hand, and he offered warmly, "Oh, I've heard all about you. You're doing such great things in the theatre. And how old is that little girl of yours now?"

Yogi always found the balance between going to church and having a gay son. She would grumble to me, "They don't understand." And add, "If they had a gay son, they'd see things differently." She was not afraid to tell the world about me, my husband, and her grandchild.

I am grateful, then, to the Catholic Church, for giving my beloved mother the great gift of faith in a powerful and loving God.

My mom died at the age of eighty-one. The priest at her

church in her final years of life was Father Graham Keep. As luck would have it, Graham and I went to high school together. We were friends in our teenage years; he acted in my plays, and we went to drinking parties together. Of course, all that happened before he was called to the ministry. Mom told Graham and me that she did in fact get the priest in the family she always wanted—it just turned out to be Graham. He was also the one to preside over my mom's funeral.

A few days before she died, she was moved into a hospital. Her body was starting to shut down, and she was bedridden. I was across the country in Vancouver, directing a play, and stopped rehearsals, bought a plane ticket, and arranged to come east to be with her. Mom's energy was dwindling, but she always had a bright clear mind, so I was able to call her at her hospital bed to tell her that I was on my way. We talked and laughed together for a couple of minutes. Then she went silent.

"Son, I'm feeling tired now. I need to rest," she said. "But I just want you to know that you have always been the sunshine of my life."

Those would be the last words she ever spoke to me. As I was making my way to the airport, she died.

My mom was known for most of her life as Yogi Garnhum. I like her baptismal name much, much more. She was baptized in the Catholic Church as Huguette Paradis. Such a beautiful name: Paradis.

Maybe I never really abandoned God: it was just the Church I lost faith in along the way. What I do know, and am feeling now, is that I have faith that Huguette, my mom, is now in paradise and with God. And that's a beautiful, reassuring feeling.

WHEN I LEAVE THE PRAYER SERVICE and emerge back into the courtyard of the monastery, the storm has completely passed. A post-storm calm, one gigantic sigh, fills the air. We are restored.

I take in a huge breath, feeling this calm inside me as well.

I find my way back through the maze to the dining hall. Walking in, I see a church dinner in full operation. Homemade food served by volunteers is presented: salads, fish, and fruit for dessert. And their homemade wine. The few people staying here barely fill up two tables. The time together is quick and polite as I share my pilgrim stories with some very kind people who are staying here for religious reasons. I am the only pilgrim in attendance tonight.

The *hospitalario* approaches me at dinner to tell me that breakfast will happen for me tomorrow at six in the morning after all. He's managed to make it work. I'm impressed and truly surprised. I thank him profusely, and he bursts into a beautiful smile of relief.

Early the next morning, as I walk through the dark courtyards lit only by a full sky of stars, I enter the cavernous dining hall. Sitting on a table is a carafe of hot coffee and a pitcher of warm milk; my place is nicely set. A basket of warm bread rolls awaits. A man I've never seen before has just finished setting the table; he gently asks me to "turn out the lights when you are done" and disappears. I sit in this place alone in the complete silence of early morning. There is seating for two hundred people to eat, but today there is just one—me. I drink my coffee and enjoy this blessed act of generosity.

I head back to my room in the dark to pick up Gregory. He and I walk through the empty maze; it is as if we are the only ones here. As I leave the monastery still in the darkness, pulling the gigantic wrought-iron metal gates closed, I feel very small against this enormous edifice.

I'm about to walk my longest day, a daunting forty kilometres.

But I'm not concerned.

Buoyed by the last fourteen hours, I have faith: in myself and, for the first time in a long, long while, for my future.

FORTY KILOMETRES OR BUST

IN ORDER TO GET A PCR COVID TEST in time to get the results and be allowed to get on the plane back to Canada, I have to speed up my timeline a bit. Tomorrow I have a noon appointment to pay a serious amount of money for someone to stick a Q-tip up my nose. If I don't make that timeline, I won't make my plane two days later. So today I will walk forty kilometres from the monastery in Sobrado to the town of O Pedrouzo, the longest distance I have ever travelled on foot in one day. If I can achieve that, then it means that I will only have a twenty-kilometre walk into Santiago tomorrow and I'll arrive on time for my Q-tip appointment.

Departing after my breakfast at six in the morning, I know I have about two hours before the sun will come up. My mighty little headlamp at the ready, I proceed down some dirt roads soaked by last night's thunderstorm. This is the first time I have walked for such an extended time in the dark all alone. Previously, walking without the benefit of the sun included ambient street light and the villages up ahead to help guide the way—making it less daunting. But today, as I head out of the village, the cloud cover combined with thicker forests and no streetlights make me nervous. Walking in the forested patches feels quite haunted and spooky. And walking on the dirt road requires focus to avoid the potholes filled with water. For the first two hours, only eight cars go by—sometimes lighting my way—giving me a hint of the road up ahead. I also have to make sure they see me coming, with very little shoulder room on the side of the road for me to escape to. I don't want to get hit—not after walking this far!

I'm getting used to unusual, scary things becoming less unusual, less scary.

There are a few lightning strikes in the distance as I go, but so far no rain. It's a relief as the sun comes up—I cheer aloud at the first sign of the sun—and the way in front of me becomes clear at last.

I decide that I will conquer this day no matter what the weather or my body suggests.

Elana would often chant to us "mind over matter" when it came to difficult walking or the threat of rain. She would say "no rain, no rain," and it was miraculous how often it worked. In the play *Room*, Ma has a charming variation on this phrase. She says, "If you don't mind," and Jack chimes in with "then it doesn't matter."

One of the highlights of walking through the province of Galicia is moving past the many dairy farms. Milk cows dominate the landscape. I stop by one of the smaller farms and sample their *queso de tetilla*. It's an aged semisoft cheese made with the milk of Galician blonde cows. It's a funny shape: pear-like with a pointed top (that's why it's called *"tetilla,"* which means "nipple" in Spanish). Convinced by my sample, I buy one pointed little ball of cheese. Its buttery taste will enliven my lunches for the next couple of days.

There has only been one threat that seriously concerned me on this Camino. And that is the presence of dogs. I've never been comfortable around them, and on this walk I must have crossed the paths of hundreds. Everyone here has a dog as a source of protection. And they all bark. Loudly. And when one dog hears a bark, they all howl, causing a chorus of noise. Often they rush toward me while aggressively barking. My first impulse is to look for the leash. And then seeing a chain, I can relax. Some of the sweet ones trick me and lie down in the middle of the road, without a leash. As I pass by them, they barely move, as if to say, *You ain't scared of little old me, are ya?*

This close to the end of the Camino, I have the mistaken belief that I'm safe. But today two dogs come toward me, off-leash and howling in full force. The small one looks harmless enough, but the bigger one has very evil eyes—eyes that say, *I'm going to bite you on the leg.* Talking calmly usually distracts them and the threat lessens quickly. Not today. This angry dog, a Spanish mastiff whose chief job is to protect his livestock, growls with intensity. He increases his volume and is marking his territory. He starts taunting me by running back and forth as I walk past. He won't let up. My heart starts to race. Where is the owner? Is his bark worse than his bite? Is he going to take a chunk out of my leg, on the penultimate day of my thirty-two days of hiking? Am I off to the hospital instead of a church in Santiago? Will I have blood rolling down my leg in a matter of minutes? How will I protect myself—my pole in my hand being my only weapon? My attempts at speaking soothingly are barely heard over his noise. I pick up my pace, and just as fast as he began barking, he turns around and runs back to his farm. His mission is complete, and my leg is spared.

Note to self: attempt to understand dogs better for more confidence in future encounters and keep a few treats at the ready.

I HAVE BEEN WARNED ABOUT TODAY: I will be joining the superhighway as the del Norte merges with the Francés. My friend Steve, a veteran of the Camino, wrote me yesterday and cautioned me not to lose myself as I merge with a sea of pilgrims all headed in the same direction. "Stay on your journey and don't feel the sense of competition to rush to the end," he wisely advised.

The merging begins upon arrival in the town of Azura, and the difference is immediate. There are pilgrims everywhere. I look around and can see thirty of them—approximately twenty-five more than usual. It's bustling with people and backpacks. Signs and billboards are directly preaching to pilgrims. And the accommodations, grocery stores, and laundromat all seem to be lined up directly on the Camino path. As I walk out of Azura and toward the next village, I notice cafés that are more like pop-up garden parties. Clearly they're created for the pilgrims and only the pilgrims. I won't have to stray far or go off the path ever, or so it seems. A beer garden I pass is particularly inviting. It reminds me of when I couldn't find food or drink of any kind for an entire day. Here on the Camino Francés, pilgrims are well cared for.

The people walking are a different mix. I hear more English spoken in my first hour on the Camino Francés than I have in the last month. I see more running shoes and fewer hiking boots. One woman I pass is wearing very revealing short shorts and thin running shoes. She is preoccupied with taking selfie photos with trees. She stops, hugs a tree, puts on a fake smile, and takes a photo of herself with the tree. She then runs to the next tree and repeats the process.

It's safe to say I'm not on the Camino del Norte anymore.

It feels like a boutique experience separate from the cities the Camino is running through. On the del Norte, the pilgrims are among the locals; here, the pilgrims are the focus. Everything about this, though colourful, is off-putting to me. That is, until I think of my child, Asher, who will be twelve soon. I've been dreaming about returning with Asher and Bruce when Asher graduates high school and how the three of us would hike a piece of the Francés together. And seeing this slightly flashy version of the Camino, I'm heartened that it might help entice Asher to join us. The beer gardens and pop-up artist stalls might sweeten my offer. And by then I will be sixty and likely happy to do the stroll a bit more easily. I see the opportunity here.

All of these distractions enable me to complete my forty kilometres in exactly ten hours without incident. Not bad after all these weeks hiking and with a twenty-five-pound backpack hanging on my back. The town of O Pedrouzo is a great stop before my final day walking into Santiago. This place reminds me of an airport hotel. Everything here—literally everything—exists solely to help the pilgrim. Hotels and food and markets. That's all that is here.

As I approach my *albergue*, I see two people waving from a restaurant. Who could it be? Yeeeesssss!!! It's Marina and Elana, my Spanish friends. They are enjoying a full *menú del día*, sharing the largest piece of red veiny meat—how delicious—a bottle of Rioja, and an impossibly large tomato salad. I had imagined I would reunite with them at the finish line tomorrow, so I'm delighted to spend the last night on the path with these women as well. I join them for lunch, and we catch up on the adventures we have missed. José is ahead and has completed the Camino and is on his way home to Barcelona, while Dick is behind us by a couple of days now.

After lunch, we head to the DIA grocery store for another bottle of wine and a bag of chips. My *albergue* has an oversize balcony with views of the surrounding farmland, so we make sure the view does not go to waste. Elana schools me in Spanish wine—her favourite being a 2019 bottle of Protos Ribera del Duero, not the classic Rioja. And I discover more about these delightful women: that the two of them met in a salsa class six years ago. Apparently, the students always moved to bars after class ended, and that is where their friendship was formed. They love to ski and play paddle tennis together. They're both single, and although I would have liked to know more about their dating situation, they seem protective of opening up about this. I've noticed a peace and purity about them that I respect. What a contrast to my time with my outspoken French mates.

Elana pulls out her Camino passport. It's overflowing with stamps of all shapes and sizes recording the journey they have had—walking the second half of the Camino del Norte. I sheepishly bring out my credentials. Incomplete. I'm a rule follower, but this time I just couldn't finish the task. I found having to prove that I was here by getting stamps along the way completely annoying. I know I'm here and I know I've not skipped steps. Not one single step. But proving it in the passport was one challenge I just wasn't up to. So somewhere along the way, a few days ago, I gave up trying. This means when I arrive tomorrow in Santiago, I won't be able to qualify for a pilgrim's certificate. I won't be officially recorded in the record books. The women are clearly surprised that I didn't complete the task. I tell them that I sincerely found it too difficult. "Too difficult?" asks Elana. "No, easy peasy." For them, it clearly was.

After my wine lesson, I'm still full of energy, so I go for a stroll along the main street, soaking in the atmosphere of pilgrims collectively enjoying their last night on the Camino. Restaurant patios are full, and the sense of excitement everyone has about finishing is palpable. Newly formed groups of friends are everywhere. I should be exhausted after such a long day, but the feeling of accomplishment combined with pride in how my body has grown stronger lifts my spirits. I've discovered that the more I walk, the more I want to keep walking. The physical journey actually became easier over these thirty-one hiking days, and my feet really only ache when I rest. I've harnessed the possibilities of this fifty-three-year-old body. Even carrying Gregory now feels natural. Three weeks ago I heard that people were having their bags sent forward to the next town, allowing for a backpack-free walking day. I decided back then to reserve the right to use this service for the last week. But now I realize I have forgotten all about that. I wouldn't dare part with Gregory. I am very grateful for the role he has played in making this trip a success.

I walked forty kilometres in one day—the equivalent length of a marathon. And I have energy left over.

WALKING IN

Six in the morning.
   Darkness.
   Again, I walk.
   But this time not alone.
   So many people.
   Thirty flashlights.
   A highway of humanity in the dark.
   All headed in the same direction.
   The Cathedral of Santiago.

I'm not with Marina and Elana. They're planning to walk
slower today, the pain in Marina's knee flaring up again. We
also have an unspoken agreement that we want to walk our
last day alone. The only puzzling thing in this mass exodus
out of O Pedrouzo is a couple who pass me in the complete
darkness. I don't see them approach because they're walking
without the assistance of a light. I turn off my headlamp and
try walking in the dark to imitate them, but I can't step a metre
without my feet becoming uncertain. I find it off-putting and
dangerous. These two walk with confidence—like they are

invincible. The Polish woman from a few days ago appears in the distance, with her headlamp blaring. With a bright smile she calls across the street: "Good morning! I don't even know your name!"

"I'm Dennis—and you?"

"Julia!" she shouts proudly.

My Polish friend has a name: Julia. And it only took me nearly two weeks to learn it. And with that, Julia rushes off ahead again. It seems like an extended time with Julia was never meant to be.

The route today into Santiago involves more country walking than I would have thought. I experience a bit of everything today—sort of like the greatest hits or megamix of my journey so far: little villages, factories, highways, fields, cows, dogs, and then urban cobblestones, highways, cars speeding past. Greatest hits.

The elevation variations are minimal today; however, I find the walk enormously challenging. My legs become sore and my feet start to burn. Damn. I think my body figured it out: the walk is coming to an end. The last five weeks have caught up to me. I find my original impulses and reactions are at play today: sore feet, always checking my watch, wondering when I will get there. Did yesterday's forty kilometres have something to do with my energy lag? (Right. I should have a sore body today. Instant forgiveness.)

The walk from this point is less euphoric, and filled with tension for me. Why are there so many pilgrims? What happens to my life when I arrive? What if I don't "feel the feels" of arrival? What if I left my husband, child, and job for nothing more than a lovely holiday? I imagine I should be getting excited about the arrival, but I know that this journey will be ending in a few hours.

Stay present.

Pilot light ignited.

Walk softly.

As soon as the city of Santiago appears in the distance, the rush is on to the cathedral. I calculate it will be ninety minutes to the church square. It seems like the season finale of *The Amazing Race*. I feel the cameras on me, so I pick up my pace. Everyone's energy changes the moment the steeple of the church comes into view. Pilgrims emerge from everywhere, and when I look behind, I see them racing toward me, moving swiftly. The highway of humanity has become the autobahn. The outer city begins to morph into the old town—pavement being replaced by cobblestones, the present being swapped out for the past. The tourist shops start popping up; the word "pilgrim" is plastered on storefronts. I'm almost there.

There's one tricky corner where the arrows fail to help. We are a few hundred feet away, but half the pilgrims turn one way, while the other half goes another. I speed forward. Bouncing down the cobblestones, breathing deeply, I feel my heart begin to race.

AT ELEVEN IN THE MORNING, September 15, 2021, after:

Three flights,

Thirty-two days, and

830 kilometres of walking,

I arrive in the square and stand before the Cathedral of Santiago de Compostela.

I look up at the impressive spires of the cathedral, but before I can take any of this in, a young Italian man steps in front of my view.

"*Señor*, will you take my picture?" he asks.

I've only been here seconds, but he unknowingly steals my moment.

After a quick second, I look at him properly. I'm taken in by the enormous energy radiating from him. He's beaming as if he has just won an Olympic gold medal. Still a bit shaken

by just arriving, I take his camera as he holds his credentials certificate high in the air—for all to see. Even though he is wildly excited, this moment between us feels very personal. He's asked me to participate in his achievement. I take one shot. And of course that's all he needs—it's perfect. He floats away into the crowd—one of the happiest people I have ever encountered.

I hear the sound of spontaneous applause and look back to where I see a group of pilgrims arriving. The applause builds, and the new arrivals wave their hands in the air in triumph. One older man in the group slows, stops, and breaks down in tears, overwhelmed. His friends gather around him. The cheers of love only grow louder. The man lifts his tear-soaked face to the crowd, and after a few more moments of crying, a smile emerges and grows across his face. He is hugged over and over and over and over.

Six cyclists ride in, looking exhausted but exhilarated. They remain in perfect formation, arms stretched to the skies.

The pilgrims continue to arrive every few minutes.

I look around 360 degrees to take in the church square properly and realize there must be two hundred people here, mostly newly arrived pilgrims. They are sitting on the cobblestones, lying against their packs, resting and recovering. Some are eating their energy snacks, drinking the last of their water. Photos are being taken. A group of euphoric women are crowded together snapping pictures and laughing. The background for everyone's photos is always the same: the cathedral. It's the best evidence in the world—we have arrived.

We are here.

We did it.

Now, feet firmly planted, my bearings intact, the world around me goes quiet. My body and mind become overwhelmed with the feeling of wonder and amazement.

Standing with the cathedral behind me, I record a video

message on my camera to the real champions of my Camino: "Hi everyone! I'm here! Look, there's the church to prove it. I'm fully overwhelmed with gratitude. That's what I'm thinking about today." I start to list the people back home I'm grateful for one by one, beginning with Bruce and Asher. I acknowledge the amazing friends who have contributed to my walk. After thanking all the Canadians on the video, I welcome my new friends I've met along the Camino who have been invaluable in my journey. "Also, I would like to thank my left foot, my right foot, and actually all of my body for staying with me— especially yesterday. And lastly I want to thank my mother-in-law, Helene, for giving me the best advice of all." My voice starts to crack. "Helene, I followed your advice, and most days accomplished it. You told me to walk softly, and for thirty-two thrilling days, that's what I did. Friends, I'm coming home with a fuller heart and buckets of gratitude. See you very soon."

I'm determined to send this message immediately. I become obsessed that it has to be shared as soon as possible— people must be acknowledged and thanked while I'm standing in this square. I feel their spirits are with me—and I need them to know I made it and am thankful. I play back the video to make sure the sound works, and then it hits me: The last time I was looking at myself on-screen, I was telling the theatre staff all about my emotional failings. I was tear soaked and looked like hell.

Reviewing this new recording, I realize I recognize this guy.

I just haven't seen him for a while.

There he is: celebrating the people that he loves.

His eyes are shining.

I send off the video as quickly as I can.

I can't linger any longer: I have to rush off and take my PCR test. A quick ten-minute walk from the cathedral brings me to a stylish clinic. A saucy nurse spends five minutes with me. It's overpriced and quickly done, but I'm grateful for the privilege of travel at this time, as I head back to the square to see Marina and Elana arrive. I celebrate them and record them in many photographs, the best being the jumping jacks in the air with the cathedral, of course, in the background.

I'm exhausted.

I find my hotel, which turns out to be directly above a tasty-looking gelato shop. From my hotel window, I can see people lining up for scoops of ice cream. Chocolate. Asher would want chocolate. I start to unpack Gregory in my usual way—strewing the contents all over the room. Before I can fully complete the task, I give in to the need to crawl in bed and slide into a power nap. I'm passed out sleeping before my head hits the pillow.

Two hours later I awake, refreshed.

A text from Joy proclaims the great news—she is back hiking and heading my way. She's likely still a week or two behind, considering the slow place she has had to adopt, but she will be able to finish the Camino. I am so pleased, and relieved for her. She congratulates me on making it to the cathedral in one piece, honoured to have received my video message.

I'm now out of my costume—no backpack, no poles—so as I walk about the city, I look like a sightseer. I feel a bit like a fraud: a pilgrim in disguise as a tourist. As pilgrims continue to pour into the city, they sometimes get lost—it's a bit of a maze here. I resist the temptation on many occasions to point their way. It's important to me that they have their own experience. All streets lead to the cathedral, so I'm not worried about them never finding the finish line.

The architecture of Santiago is spectacular, and it's crowded with people on every street, down every colourful alleyway. It's the most touristy place I have been during this time in Spain. After such an adventure, I don't really mind the T-shirt and traditional cookie shops that are everywhere. It all feels like a celebration. Seeing the tour groups cluster and be guided around in tight formations is a bit of a shock though. I've spent a month immersed in the culture of northern Spain. These people are getting the quick version. (That said, the tacky, fake little white train that moves tourists through town looks like a relaxing afternoon adventure.)

Our celebration dinner is at a place Elana's friend has recommended, Restaurante María Castaña. Most restaurants in Santiago specialize in serving seafood, and I'm thrilled when Elana offers to order for us. Elana suggests that the entire meal should be made up of the traditional food of the region. It's a "feast of firsts" for me with my Spaniard friends leading the way. We begin by eating *percebes* (gooseneck barnacles). I'm taught how to suck out the good fleshy bits inside, as one does with crab. Our second course is *erizo de mar* (sea urchins) scrambled in eggs, which is incredibly salty and tart, and we finish with *pulpo a la gallega* (grilled octopus with potatoes) as the main course. I'm quite surprised by the flavour and texture. I like it. (And yes, it tastes like chicken.)

We agree to meet up one more time together—before we have to say our goodbyes. So tonight we keep it simple with "congratulations!"

As I walk to my hotel, I pass through the cathedral square: quiet, dark, and serene. Street musicians have set up where only hours ago it was filled with newly arrived pilgrims. The square must wait till tomorrow for more arrivals, I imagine. While in the square, my phone lights up, showing that I have missed a call. It's Marie from Paris. I sent her the video message earlier today. I play her voicemail, and when I hear her voice and her broken English, my heart leaps:

"I want to speak English to you so I doing a vocal message. Dennis, you did it! I'm super, super proud and super happy. I hope you're super proud of you too, because it's really a big thing that you've done. I want to say that even if we left the

Camino a few weeks ago, it was super nice to know that you are still doing it. Now I had a strange feeling when I've seen this video of you. I thought, *Oh, so now my Camino, it's really at the end.* Before I was like, *I'm doing my day in Paris and somewhere Dennis is walking, so I'm still on the Camino with him.* It was a good feeling to know that you were walking somewhere. But now it's the end, so I feel sad. But I'm happy that you made it. I hope your feet are fine. I just want to say that I'm super, super happy that we had to met you, and I hope that you will come in Paris as soon as you can, because I will be super happy to see you again." Yes, Marie: we "had to met you."

I fall asleep with visions of the people I love. Tonight they are sleeping in their beds too: in France and in Spain and, of course, my lovely humans in Canada.

BLESSINGS

I WAKE UP IN A BIT OF A DAZE at six in the morning.

My body is ready to walk.

My heart wants to walk.

But I have to take a moment and confirm: it's over.

The Camino is complete. And I'm clear that the choice of the Camino del Norte was brilliantly perfect for me: the right amount of challenge, combined with the beauty of walking ocean side.

When someone runs a marathon, they end up celebrating with their pals in a pub. Here we go to church. Currently they are offering three pilgrim masses a day in the cathedral. Seating is restricted due to COVID. If you have obtained your certificate—proof you have walked the Camino—you get a ticket to mass and enter from a separate door. For me, I have to line up with the tourists. I feel slighted, but the rules are always the rules. Next time, I promise, I will get the stamps, and I will go through the side door.

As I wait for mass to begin, I think about how strange it is that I have been in this church before. Seventeen years ago I spent a summer working with a high-end travel company called Horizon Holidays. In order to train me to be a guide, they handed me their brochure and said, "Which trip do you want to go on anywhere in the world?" I chose the most elaborate one: a two-week escorted cruise in the inaugural year of the *Queen Mary 2*. It sailed out of Southampton in England and travelled around the Mediterranean for a luxurious two weeks. I was in training, so I helped the highly experienced and lovely guide John lead twenty-five seniors on this elaborate cruise. One of our stops allowed us to get on a bus and come to the cathedral here. We saw the arrival of pilgrims and had a private tour. That was followed by a five-star lunch in a restaurant nearby. At the time, I remember thinking, *Who in the world would want to do a pilgrimage?* I was in my thirties, and this was a part-time gig on a cruise ship. And I hadn't hiked much out in the world yet. It was so far from my reality. Not something I would even consider. We watched with tourist curiosity before rushing off to lunch—food being the real highlight of all cruises.

I do remember sticks, poles, and crutches stacked throughout the church. Pilgrims would leave them inside when their journey was done. The cathedral clearly has gone through an extensive renovation—cleaning the ancient brick, installing new benches—and there are no crutches to be found. A COVID thing? Maybe.

The mass begins, and I follow along easily enough—the format is universal for Catholics, no matter the language. There is a point in the service when the priest invites the congregation to shake hands with their fellow parishioners. I know it's coming and wonder how we will do this in the time of COVID. I've always appreciated the act of acknowledging each other—it's the warmest moment of the mass for me. As a kid, it was the fun part—shaking hands with as many people as you could in thirty seconds. At the appointed time today, the priest invites us to look at each other—instead of touching. I look around, bow my head many times, and lock eyes with people all around me. It's electric having these direct connections. With a handshake, shy people tend not to look up. With this, it feels like an essential and vital moment. I can sense the smiles behind the eyes and the masks. I would call this a "COVID keep"—something enhanced or made better during COVID times.

I don't get to witness the big feature of the mass: the swinging of the *botafumeiro*. This epically large silver censer is swung back and forth over the altar during a moment in the mass; it's a mighty effort requiring the strength of a few robed monks. This *botafumeiro* is one of the largest in the world. The strong incense fills the room, and all are blessed. In the Middle Ages, it was believed that incense smoke had a protective effect at the time of plagues and epidemics. It's not guaranteed during the mass, and it needs to be sponsored through a donation. Apparently 450 euros have to be given every time in order for it to be utilized. Not at our mass today. It didn't swing for me. Another reason for me to return.

The service today is elaborate: the setting an ornate church, the players all dressed in matching regal costumes. There are scenes, songs, and processions all opulently staged and covered in glorious ornamentation—great inspiration for a theatre director.

At the end of the mass, I approach the altar. I light a candle for my mom, in the centre of the cathedral. I thank her for being with me along this journey. Today's candle lighting feels joyous and gratifying. I feel my mom's spirit watching over me saying, *You did good, son, you did good.* She's also calculating that I've been around a whole heck of a lot of spiritual places in the last few weeks. *I must have done something right,* she is saying to herself right now, with a twinkle in her eye.

Marina and Elana invite me out to another seafood extravaganza; however, I need to get to bed early tonight—I have a long travel day home tomorrow. And honestly, I don't know if I can digest another octopus. So instead, we meet up in a local pub where the main feature is an impressive collection of beer from around the world. Elana's longtime friend Alejandro joins us. He's colourful and loves to talk. Elana leans over to me and says that he is a "typical Galician man," and she offers it without comment. Our banter weaves in and out of Spanish, mostly focusing on our countries and traditions. Alejandro loves hockey, and he loves the Raptors, our Toronto basketball team. I fail, as always, in any conversation regarding sports. But I try.

When we lift our glasses to toast with our beers, I'm taught the Spanish way. It goes like this: We hold up our glasses, say something appropriate ("We did it!"), and then before anyone can drink, we MUST ensure that the glasses touch the table for one second. Then we can lift them back up and drink. If we don't do that, and proceed directly to drinking after the toast, we will have bad luck in our sex lives. We practice this a few times—I don't want this curse upon me. I'm not sure if this is a true Spanish tradition, and I don't care. I love that I'm included.

"Look at this!" Marina rolls up her sleeve and reveals a newly minted tattoo in the shape of a yellow arrow. "And mine!" says Elana, showing off her scallop-shell tattoo at her ankle. I'm jealous! I'd thought of getting a tattoo here—it would be my first. The women tell me that they booked their appointment two weeks ago; apparently, it's a very popular thing for pilgrims to do. However, Marina's tattoo artist told her they are a bit bored with sketching arrows all day long. Ha! I will book one next visit.

As our time together starts to wrap up, I look over at Marina. It's been a hard walk for her. Her knee has been acting up, and some of the asphalt walking on roads really was difficult for her. But her glow remains, and all I see is charm and promise. In the future, I want to experience the buildings that she will design. I know they will reflect her glorious spirit, her gifted creativity, and her bubbly heart. I know she will soar. I'll miss her.

Elana and I walk together as we leave the bar. We've talked a lot about our mutual language-learning difficulties. And she admits she was hesitant to talk those first few days because of her insecurities. Now we walk together doing our best with what words we have. I have seen her blossom over this past week. Elana asks me if we can stay in touch. She'd love to keep practicing her English with me. I offer that, from now on, she can only communicate with me in English and I will only communicate in Spanish. We will help each other. They've brought up the idea of coming to Canada many times. Today they ask if they can come to Toronto and ski. I laugh. Toronto is known for many things—but not for skiing. We still have so much to discover about each other. I welcome the opportunity.

As we hug goodbye, I think of these ambassadors of Spain as another reminder of what is possible on a Camino. I love my new friends from around the world, and these Spaniards have given me such a gift—to see the Camino through their effervescent, kind, local eyes.

I can't resist one last walk to cathedral square so that I can say goodbye and thank you to the magnificent church, my goal for the last five weeks. While there, a feeling floats into my heart: it's time to go home.

HOMEWARD

IT'S MID-SEPTEMBER NOW. STUDENTS are back to school, the beaches are empty, and fall's cooler temperatures have begun to settle in. My trip back to Canada won't be as arduous as my trip over. The flights are much better organized this time, without lengthy stopovers, and I'll be home in time to kiss the kid good night.

Experienced pilgrims warn the new ones: the reentry back into the real world is jarring. In the early morning in Santiago, I step into a taxi—the first mode of transport in over thirty days. The car seems to be travelling fast; my eyes need to adjust to this speedy mode of travel. I arrive at the shiny new Santiago–Rosalía de Castro Airport, and the formality of it all feels strange. My body still connects early morning darkness with walking. But instead I'm checking in my knapsack for my flight. Gregory will be travelling with the other baggage today, not on my back. I place him on the conveyor belt and feel a true sense of loss.

Trying to engage with the Iberia check-in person, I tell her that Gregory has been on my back for five weeks and I'll miss him today. I say it with a devilish grin.

I wait. Nothing. Not an ounce of acknowledgment.

Then I gleefully state, "I just finished walking the Camino de Santiago."

Nothing.

I'm the only person in line, the airport empty, but this woman doesn't want to engage. Hopping over to a fancy little coffee shop by the departure gate for my last breakfast in Spain, I'm startled to see that the prices are three times as much as on the Camino. And the coffee is not nearly as tasty.

Welcome back to the real world.

My first flight takes me to the Madrid airport, where I first touched ground in Spain. As I depart the plane and enter the terminal, I'm delighted to see that the place is starting to come back to life—more than it was five weeks ago. While still not to capacity, the number of people here is encouraging. It now looks more full than empty: people pack the benches, waiting for their flights to take off. It seems like a gift of reassurance: it's time for all of us to get on with our lives.

While the Madrid airport feels like the beginning steps toward normalcy, Heathrow Airport in London, England, is crowded and full of frantic passengers racing through. It's frenetic—just like the old days. It looks and feels as if there's never been a pandemic here. I don't know if that's a good thing or not.

I'm finished with my Spanish words for now, back in an English-speaking culture. I'll miss hearing my valiant attempts at Spanish coming out of my mouth. As I look around the airport—people racing to their flights, customers lining up for food—I scan faces and look at people's luggage: there isn't a pilgrim to be seen anywhere.

I squeeze into my seat on this full British Airways flight to Canada; with the exception of the masks that all are wearing, everything feels normal.

But it's not normal for me.

Something has changed.

I'm feeling pretty chill.

Relaxed.

Calm.

Cool.

Peaceful.

I'm coming to realize that it doesn't matter whatsoever what I do with the rest of my life. What matters is how I live the rest of my life.

I need to "walk softly."
"Welcome" everyone.
"Move forward" toward beauty.
And "push" away fear.

In these 250 hours of mostly silent walking, I have had time to:

Ask myself big life questions.
Challenge myself to be better.
Be frustrated with myself for the mistakes I have made.
Love myself for pursuing my passions.

I've laughed at full volume with only myself to hear.
Called myself "idiot" in the middle of a farmer's field.
Skipped over puddles while balancing my backpack.
Danced naked in the ocean.
I've fallen and cut my knee.
And I've soared.

What it all seems to come down to is that:

My heart has been broken.

And what's most disturbing to me is that I've finally come to realize:

I'm the one who broke it.

No one else.

At my best, I live in semi-innocent and naive boy-like wonder. As things came crashing down around me over these past months, I abandoned hope and stopped trusting that little boy inside me. I gave up on him. He liked to say silly things, come up with goofy ideas, and fall in love with almost every good person he's ever met. But the fantastic news is I've had a glimpse of that boy returning on this journey. Somewhere along the path this last week—I can't pinpoint when—he appeared to me again. He whispered in my ear:

You have been strong before.
And you will be strong again soon.

I came on this Camino to justify the end of my life of creativity and to allow myself to run away and hide. It seems like that version is not to be. This pandemic has helped me to rediscover the brighter creative world out there with so many more avenues to offer. The boy inside me who once spent hours creating a puppet show in his basement has been seen bouncing along an 830-kilometre road with joyful ease.

He's been let free once again to:

Dance,
Sing,
Skinny dip,
Giggle, and
Dream.

A F T E R

REENTRY

I STEP TOWARD A FAMILIAR FACE in the Toronto airport: Bruce opens his arms wide as I approach him. His spirit is infectious, and I easily slide into his waiting arms.

"You did it," Bruce whispers into my ear.

Bruce tosses my pack into the back seat of our RAV4, and we head home. Having no idea where to start a conversation—there's so much to say—we chatter on about the flight, COVID protocols, and airplane food. When we arrive home, I can hear Asher playing *Minecraft*, a video game, with their friend Mimi in the basement.

"Daddy's home!" I call out.

"Daaaaaaaddy!" Asher screams as they bounce up the stairs.

They've grown taller.

And what a sight: I'm caught by their energy and innocence. And their beauty. "Hey, Asher," I call out, trying on their new name for the first time. "I've missed you!"

We have a squeezy, silly, intimate hug.

"What did you bring me?" Asher jumps to it. I toss them

a skull-and-crossbones T-shirt with a radical Camino logo across it.

"Cool!" they shout. I nailed it. And with that they race back to the game in progress downstairs.

BRUCE HAS BROUGHT OUT SOME WINE and cheese for the two of us (mostly for me). He wants to hear every detail about the journey. I've been waiting to share my stories with him, so I jump in and slowly walk through the days in too much detail, show him the 350 photographs on my camera, and give him the very long version of what is bubbling up inside me.

He listens,

And listens,

And listens,

And listens.

About an hour into regaling him with yet another story, I realize that I am staring across at the same old Bruce I left five weeks ago. And that is a very comforting thing. While my emotions tend to run me, Bruce has always been a grounding force. He has a glow about him tonight: I can feel his pride.

"Did you ever worry about me, Bruce?" I asked.

"On the Camino? Nope. Not once. I've worried for you many times over this last year, but the moment you set off, I knew you'd ace the Camino."

"Will you hike the Dolomites in Italy with me next summer?" I ask.

"It would be my pleasure," Bruce says. "If you think I can keep up."

The next Monday, driving to the theatre, my senses are jolted. I find the drive incredibly stressful, and noisy. It certainly isn't a walk down a country road. I park my car and walk to the building, my heart pounding. What am I about to encounter? Putting on a brave face, I step into the theatre.

The energy's electric as I pass through the stage door—

unlike anything I have experienced in the last eighteen months here. There are people in the building doing their regular theatre jobs. Walking into Deb's office, I find that my hope for a big hug and an "I've missed you" is short lived. An emergency meeting is in progress. One of the artists we've had on contract has been accused of misconduct. Something has to be done. The conversation is about firing this person. Deb says with an apologetic grin, "Welcome home."

I walk down the theatre hallways and staff members call out kind words; however, "welcome back" doesn't have quite the same power as *"buen Camino."* A newer staff member asks me how my vacation was (vacation?). But mostly, everyone is focused on work. By the end of the day, I have learned about the trials and tribulations that I have missed over five weeks. The focus here is around all the stress associated with coming back to work during this pandemic, and the concerns about reopening our theatre. I don't share one story with anyone today. I am being sucked right back into a busy work world.

On my second day back at work, Deb and I go for a walk. I am prepared to hear a long list of the problems associated with the theatre. Mostly I am waiting to learn about the big bombs that went off during my absence that they kept from me. As we begin our walk along the Thames River, Deb reveals, "I have nothing to report—I just want to hear all about your Camino." My heart leaps, and the stories flow out of me. I don't stop talking for two hours.

When I left for the Camino, our renovation was half-finished, the lobby spaces having been ripped down to the studs. For months a ghostlike, industrial emptiness defined our lobby. At the end of the workday, when everyone has left, I put on a yellow hard hat and my steel-toed boots. I make my way quietly to the lobby, push back a heavy plastic tarp, and crawl through. Stepping into the newly renovated lounge, I am taken by the bright, fresh, modern look. The lengthy new bar is lit up with hi-tech LED lighting, making it glow red from within. The removal of walls has had a dramatic effect on the room: our city view has expanded. And directly in sight across the street is St. Peter's Cathedral. I was a choirboy there, singing on Sundays as a child. I've never given that much thought, but now I delight in this gentle reminder of all the cathedrals in Spain. This cathedral here in London will be a touchstone for me.

Returning to the Grand and seeing it renovated throughout is a notion not lost on me: my restoration took place on a walk in Spain, this one through paint, bricks, and glass. I hope we are both ready for our next phase.

As I return to my daily theatre life, when things start ramping up and feeling stressful, I summon my inner Camino and share with my colleagues that I have made a promise to myself: I am keeping my Camino zen for as long as possible. "Let's pause, breathe, and take it slow," I say often to unsuspecting coworkers. They put up with me during these first weeks after my return. Anita, the board chair who supported my time away, drops by the theatre to offer me a warm "welcome back" that speaks volumes of support and compassion.

I chat with one of our scenic painters, Craig, as he welcomes me home. I tell him about the Guggenheim in Bilbao, how he would love it, and how it reminded me of the power of art to restore. Craig tells me, "I've never had a time when I felt bad that I didn't rescue myself with art." Wise words. It just took me a strenuous five-week hike across Spain to understand that.

GRAND REOPENING

WHILE IN THEATRE MEETINGS, I'm no longer distracted by thoughts of picnics with my sore feet dangling in cold streams. And yet I am still feeling great peace within. I suspect that this is the "Camino effect" working on me. Joy told me that people receive the true gift of the Camino over time. For most it happens on the walk, but for many it happens months later. For me a tangible impact is beginning to emerge now, two months after coming back from Spain. Through practice and trial and error, I've been reinforcing my Camino insights, and they are becoming new life principles—the words "walk softly" guide most of my steps still. But it does take time.

Every couple of weeks since I've been home, something will set me off. And I'll feel myself inviting insecurities to walk back in. But so far I've been able to sound the alarms to myself: stop and breathe. And I force myself to stay on this new path I'm carving out. "I'm not going backward," I tell myself adamantly. As hard as it is to freeze the moment and pivot back to joy, I've been able to do it.

• • •

I AM STRIVING TO:
> Look for pleasure in the uncertainty.
> Face the unknown future with the heart of a pilgrim.
> Remain wide-eyed throughout the day.
> Take in the full panorama of life.
> Revel in amazement.
> Be curious.
> Move toward beauty.

REOPENING A THEATRE DURING pandemic times is terribly complicated, stressful, and challenging since new protocols have to be established. It's a crash course in safety for us all: vaccine passports, scanning patrons at entryways, spacing out seating assignments, stocking sanitizers and masks throughout the building. Our meetings result in more rules, a larger workload for the entire staff, and of course increased pressure to keep healthy. I'm finding, however, that I don't mind all the logistics, and more importantly, I'm working on keeping emotions (mine and everyone else's) as calm and relaxed as possible.

Through this time, we've worked out the construction kinks and have been implementing the new toys that have been added during the renovation. (Can we figure out the controls for the three hundred LED colours available now in the lobby lighting? How do you explain "all-gender washrooms" to patrons who are resistant to change? Will the new lobby furniture arrive in time, given the problems with delivery worldwide?)

ON THE TWENTY-FOURTH OF NOVEMBER, we raise the curtain on the completion of the nine-million-dollar renovation. Three hundred press, sponsors, staff, and tradespeople are sitting together onstage with the curtain down, facing the auditorium. The board chair, lead sponsors, Deb, and architects take turns acknowledging the key players. When Ron, a valued board member, speaks from the podium, he talks of my vision for the project. His words are generous. I am caught totally off guard. I must have made a gesture or had a very shocked look on my face because Ron looks at me and says, "You seem surprised by my words, Dennis. Don't be." In front of the captive crowd. I somehow forgot that I've been a part of this project for three years.

It's my turn. I approach the podium, and with a touch of theatrical flair, I call for our crew members to stand by. I ask Steve, a loyal employee with thirty years of experience, to ready the team.

"Aaron, sound cue one: GO!"

Olympian-themed music begins to play.

"Wright, lighting cue one: GO!"

The stage fades to black.

I'm speaking in a full voice now:

"Jarod, fly cue one, plus sound cue two and lighting cue two: GO!"

This command causes our main curtain to rise slowly and gracefully as the music swells, revealing our spectacular auditorium of empty seats with hundreds of helium-filled gold balloons attached to them. For us, they represent the people we envision returning to our theatre in the upcoming months. We invite the audience to wander our brand-new spacious lobbies and celebrate the completion of the renovation of the Grand. Copious champagne is poured, confetti cannons shoot paper into the air, and with that, the Grand Theatre is reopened.

Over the next few months, smaller projects, including a holiday concert, are mounted in our theatre to slowly and safely invite our audiences back in and to show off the renovation. But the highlight, coming early next year, will be to finally open *Room* after an incredible, unprecedented two-year delay.

OPENING NIGHT

I awake this morning and look at myself in the mirror—my recent attempt at growing a beard is a resounding success. I had never really tried before; however, a few weeks ago, I was about to shave off the scrubby bits when a new colleague, Saccha, told me how much she liked it and that I should keep it. So I have. I see things in the beard I have never seen before: grays and whites and various shades of brown. The mosaic is unexpected, and I enjoy this look.

The response was initially mixed. Deb wondered why I was growing a beard now, when I could have had one on the Camino and gotten it over with. Bruce likes it—calling it "dashing." Denise in the box office tells me her eighty-year-old mother saw a picture of me recently and says it makes me look younger. I wonder if that's the beard at play, or something more? I enjoy distracting everyone and myself with this whimsy. Of the things that people didn't expect of me, I add this to the list. Staring at my redefined facial features, I think about today and I whisper to myself, "It's happening."

After two long years of waiting, we will finally have that opening night.

In twelve hours we'll open what I affectionately have dubbed *Room* 3.0. After the cancellation two years ago, we had intended to reopen it (*Room* 2.0) in January 2022. After that long suspension, the artists returned this past December to prepare for the show all over again.

Rehearsals were intense: actors walking into the building happy but fearful. The pressure of "getting it right" after such a long time away was causing them self-doubt. They rehearsed the play with masks on their faces—trying to connect to the other actors across the room. It was difficult to hear words through the masks, so subtlety while acting was on pause. After rapid tests for everyone in the rehearsal to confirm a negative COVID status, the masks came off. These vulnerable, gifted actors began to shine: they could see each other's reactions, receive their glowing faces. Emotions remained raw though. The joy of returning was combined with sudden bursts of tears at the pressure and confusion of being back.

Just as the cast of *Room* 2.0 was becoming confident and opening night approached, the Omicron variant that was taking over the world meant that we had to shut down the production for a second time. It was devastating to the cast who had managed to relearn the entire play. The day we cancelled *Room* 2.0, the twenty-six-foot moving truck filled with two-year-old scenery was headed back to the theatre. The rules in Ontario stated that large gatherings were forbidden once again. We laid off the company for a second time.

Unlike in some other businesses where craftspeople can switch to another project, there was nothing else to offer them. Artists went home and waited. Deb and I decided we couldn't postpone this play indefinitely again. So instead of cancelling it, we moved two new productions about to go into rehearsal out of the season. We put the *Room* setup on our stage immediately, with only a faint hope that, in fact, we would return. The next performance in this theatre's history would be the opening of *Room*, we decided. That was our resolve. Our staff stayed home, and the theatre went empty all over again. The sparkling new renovation was being appreciated by no one. This second shutdown was markedly different for me, however. This time I didn't break down or take it personally. Quite the opposite—I rose to the challenge. And at least we knew the routine.

After this hiatus, we all returned three weeks ago and quickly finished what we started. Last night was the final preview in front of an audience for this 3.0 version. We are ready.

WHILE I'M STILL ADMIRING MY NEW FACIAL HAIR, Bruce calls Asher and me into the kitchen. He holds up the *Globe and Mail* national newspaper. I have a feeling I know what's inside. He opens the paper, turning to page B5. Together the three of us look at a full-page article, complete with pictures, celebrating the work of the Grand Theatre.

In the most fortuitous timing, Kelly Nestruck, arts reporter for the *Globe*, had been wanting to write a story about the Grand, the renovation, and its leadership for a few years—that article having been put on pause two years ago thanks to the pandemic. Kelly picked up where he had left off and travelled to the Grand through a mini-snowstorm to interview our team over a three-hour period a few weeks ago. "London's Grand Theatre has grand plans" blares the headline, with the subhead "Dennis Garnhum is back remaking the once-staid regional theatre company into one that embraces the new and unexpected." And Deb and I are there together in a photograph, beaming (with my new beard on proud display).

During our interview, Kelly mentioned to me that I had a quieter demeanour than he remembered. I paused for a moment. Do I tell him? In a quiet voice, I shared with him that I had a breakdown last summer, ran off to the Camino de Santiago, and returned a more chill and calm person. "I'm sorry to hear that, Dennis," he kindly offered. "I can't imagine what it was like for people in your position to have to unhire artists and unproduce shows."

I hadn't thought of going public but decided that if he was going to write about our success at this time, we also had to come clean about the cost for all of us. I wasn't afraid of how he would capture this in the newspaper. However, when I read his reference to my breakdown, I tear up. A year ago I was in a terribly dark place, convinced I was done with theatre forever, and this morning I am reading my comments about "grand plans" in a national paper. It boggles my mind.

And most importantly, it's just information.

Asher says, "Cool, Dad. I have to get to school." And off they go. Bruce gives me a big hug.

I dash off to the theatre.

We are hosting a staff breakfast meeting this morning. As our staff enters the renovated lounge, the buffet is set: eggs, bacon, sausage, tomatoes, muffins, yogurt, coffee, tea, and juice. Deb and I are behind the bar serving breakfast: it's a promise we made two years ago—that when we returned, Deb and I would head into the kitchen. As they fill their plates, I'm improvising a whole bunch of lies about how Deb and I have spent the entire night frying the bacon and scrambling the eggs. My improv becomes more elaborate: "I cut my finger chopping the potatoes, so watch out for blood. . . ." The staff plays along, knowing full well that Deb and I hate to cook— even postpandemic. Our development director Suzanne and her dedicated associate Grace to the rescue—they brought breakfast back to the Grand.

Deb and I step onto the freshly renovated concert stage in our lounge. We begin with a toast:

"To the opening night of *Room* 3.0!" Deb offers. Coffee mugs are raised.

"To *Room* 3.0," everyone speaks in unison. Cheers of joy fill the room.

"It's time to move forward," I say. The staff nod in agreement.

The afternoon is busy with one last rehearsal to fine tune the ending sequence of the play and to calm the nerves of the actors as they warm up for their opening night. As I check in on departments throughout the building, I am peaceful. Lyndee, the producer, tells me she hopes tonight happens and knocks wood. I tell her not to worry, it will happen. She winks in agreement. The cast do a rapid test this afternoon— fearful that if anyone tests positive, the opening night will be cancelled. Everyone is negative. It's the only time "negative" is a good word.

I KEEP CHECKING MY WATCH.

Five in the afternoon.

Nerves kick in.

Is this finally going to happen?

AT EXACTLY EIGHT IN THE EVENING, Deb and I step in front of the curtain. We're sold out tonight, and what has been a sea of red velvet chairs for far too long is now taken over with familiar faces beaming back at us. The audience begins to ap-plaud as we introduce ourselves, and very quickly the entire audience rises to their feet. A standing ovation is a sight to behold and be a recipient of. Everyone is thrilled to be here tonight.

We welcome everyone back and assure them that we are, finally, minutes away from beginning *Room* 3.0. I publicly ac-knowledge that Emma Donoghue and her family are with us. Deb reveals to the audience that we will be announcing next year's season shortly—an impressive lineup of ten productions and four world premieres with our theme of "LIVE! and in Person."

Act 1 goes smoothy: the actors are electric. Alexis Gordon playing Ma is on fire—fully present and pouring her heart into this demanding role. The laugher early on is one of recognition; the play grows more quietly as the tragedy of confinement sets in. At intermission, I see Quinsley in the audience, the boy who played Jack the first time. He's grown in these two years—as boys do—so we had to recast the part. I notice he's wiping away tears as I approach him. It's a bittersweet night for the young man. He never got to finish what he started. In act 2, Ma and Jack are in the world now, having escaped. An early scene in a hospital where Ma's mother wears a mask is received with a couple of awkward chuckles—it's all too familiar.

There are no easy answers, outside of this room, this play suggests. Getting out is the first task; finding your way forward is the ultimate one. As I sit in the darkened theatre, I am reminded of why this play continued to haunt me on my Camino journey. All the confining spaces I have freed myself from— the sad childhood, the Catholic shame, the personal attacks. And just recently I worked through my own personal pain of thinking my creative days were over. I got out, and now I face the work of finding my way forward.

In the final scene, Jack, now played by a bright boy named Lucien, asks Ma if he can return to where they were held captive one last time. At first alarmed by this idea, Ma then agrees. As they step through the door, and into the room, they revisit the everyday objects that helped them survive. Part of their ritual every morning when they were trapped would be to say hello to each item. One by one. And now, instead, they say goodbye.

"Goodbye, lamp."

"Goodbye, wardrobe."

"Goodbye, sock puppet."

"Goodbye, skylight."

As they go through their list, I go through mine:

Goodbye, fear.

Goodbye, doubts.

Goodbye, pain.

Goodbye, pandemic.

Ma finishes the play by saying, "We take one last look . . . and walk right out the door."

In these final minutes, I can hear people in the audience crying all around me. As the lights come up for the bow, the audience jumps to their feet for a second time tonight, wiping their eyes as they stand.

I STAY AT THE OPENING-NIGHT PARTY until two in the morning, my family having gone home a few hours earlier. As the party winds down, I step outside the front doors of the theatre and look up and down Richmond Street—there's no one around. Only fresh falling snow. I am all alone. As I begin moving toward home, I realize this all feels familiar—walking in the dark with only my thoughts to accompany me. This opening night solidifies it: I'm destined for an artistic life, be it in a theatre or otherwise. I pass by St. Peter's Cathedral, my childhood church, and I am reminded of my visit to the monastery where I found a renewed faith in myself and the next steps I want to take in my life.

The me of my childhood and the me of now will find a place and purpose in the world again. The Camino taught me that. With my late-night walk coming to a close, and my home now in sight, I think of the final hours of my Camino and the cathedral in Santiago.

◆ ◆ ◆

ON MY LAST DAY IN SPAIN, six months ago, I walked back into cathedral square after going to mass. I sat down in the middle of hundreds of pilgrims and took out the rock. I had considered many places for leaving the little thing. Many times I had walked by rock piles created by other passing pilgrims where I could've left it. But in the moment, it hadn't seemed right. One idea I had was that, wherever I left the rock, I would record its location carefully, and when I brought my family back to Spain, we would find it together. I liked the idea of controlling and directing the rock's story. However, on my Camino journey, I finally understood that it is ok to let things go, to trust in the way, and to honour what is.

With that in mind, I decided to leave the rock, and all my remaining sorrows, in the middle of the square.

The fate of the rock belonged to the rock now.

I bent down and placed it in a crack between two cobblestones, among the hundreds of pilgrims who were gathered and unaware of what I was up to. I stood up and walked away, releasing the rock and all that it had held for me, forever.

Goodbye, rock.

Maybe someone will see the rock and claim it as their own. Maybe a cleaner will sweep it away. When we go back, if we go back, it might be there—somewhere in Spain.

I've come to realize that knowing that is enough.

ACKNOWLEDGMENTS

FOR ONE PERSON TO walk solo and record these thoughts, it required a bountiful, kind, and generous collection of beautiful people:

Bruce Sellery, Asher Sellery, Helene Sellery, Cindy Denomme, Guy Beaudin, Deb Harvey, Suzanne Lanthier, Caitlin Core, Kirk Austensen, Lesley MacMillan, Bretta Gerecke, Cameron Carver, Jesse Finklelstein, Amanda Lewis, Christina Henry de Tessan, Guillermo Galvan Goo, Gali Kronenberg, Gail Hudson, Paul Barrett, Emilie Sandoz-Voyer, Katie Meyers, Elayne Becker, Scott McKowen, Jen Mactaggart, Steve Hartwell, Tracey Ferencz, Anita Shah, Michael Milde, and Aara Suksi.

Special thanks to the staff and board of directors of the Grand Theatre, the company of *Room*, and my fellow pilgrims: Joy, Marie, Nicolas, Pierre, Paulo, Marina, Elana, José, Dick, Valentino, and Julia.

And of course to my left foot, my right foot, and Sebastián.

ABOUT THE AUTHOR

 DENNIS GARNHUM IS A writer, a theatre director, and the artistic director of the Grand Theatre in London, Canada. Before that, he was the artistic director of Theatre Calgary between 2005 and 2016. In addition to directing at those theatres, he has been a guest director of productions for Bangkok University in Thailand and for companies which include the Stratford Festival, Shaw Festival, Canadian Stage, American Conservatory Theater, Vancouver Opera, National Arts Centre, Tarragon Theatre, Royal Manitoba Theatre Centre, Florida Grand Opera, Bard on the Beach, and Citadel Theatre. Garnhum is a recipient of the Queen Elizabeth II Diamond Jubilee Medal. He has written and cowritten several award-winning plays and adaptations, including *Lost: A Memoir*, *Timothy Findley's The Wars*, and *A Christmas Carol*. *Toward Beauty* is his first book. He lives in Ontario with his family.

ABOUT THE ILLUSTRATOR

SCOTT MCKOWEN IS AN award-winning illustrator and graphic designer. American born, he lives in Stratford, Ontario, where he operates the design studio Punch & Judy Inc. with his partner, theatre designer Christina Poddubiuk. McKowen has created theatre posters for plays by Shakespeare, Shaw, Chekhov, and Molière, as well as works by contemporary playwrights for theatre companies across North America. He has illustrated books by Lewis Carroll, Mark Twain, Jonathan Swift, Jules Verne, Washington Irving, Edgar Allen Poe, Oscar Hijuelos, Jane Urquhart, Gregory Maguire, and Neil Gaiman. *Light Revealed: Scratchboard Engravings by Scott McKowen* and *How I Draw: Scott McKowen Sketchbooks* are both available from Firefly Books.